HATCHMENTS IN BRITAIN

2

Norfolk and Suffolk

2
Norfolk
and
Suffolk

Edited by

PETER SUMMERS, F.S.A.

PHILLIMORE

1976

Published by

PHILLIMORE & CO. LTD.

London & Chichester

Head Office: Shopwyke Hall

Chichester, Sussex, England

ISBN 0 85033 230 3

PRINTED AND BOUND BY
W AND J MACKAY LTD

CONTENTS

General Introduction   ix

Abbreviations   xiv

Norfolk   1

Suffolk   63

ILLUSTRATIONS

page

NORFOLK

Snettisham: For Henry Styleman, 1819   2

SUFFOLK

Long Melford: For Thomas, 1st Viscount Savage, 1635 ...   64

GENERAL INTRODUCTION

Hatchments are a familiar sight to all those who visit our parish churches. They are not only decorative, but of great interest to the herald, genealogist and local historian. It is therefore surprising that — apart from local surveys in a few counties mostly in recent years — no attempt has yet been made to record them on a national scale. This series will, it is hoped, remedy the deficiency; it is proposed to publish separate volumes covering all English counties as well as Wales, Scotland and Ireland.

It is probable that no volume will be complete. Previously unrecorded hatchments will turn up from time to time; many have already been found in obscure places such as locked cupboards and ringing chambers. There are likely to be some inaccuracies, for hatchments are often hung high up in dark corners, and the colours may have faded or be darkened with age and grime. Identification is a problem if the arms do not appear anywhere in print: and even if the arms are identified, pedigrees of the family may not always be available. But enough has been done to make publication worth while; the margin to the pages will perhaps allow for pencilled amendments and notes.

Since I began the survey in 1952 many hatchments, probably evicted at the time of Victorian restorations, have been replaced in the churches whence they came. On the other hand, during the same period just as many hatchments have been destroyed. An excuse often made by incumbents is that they are too far gone to repair, or that the cost of restoration is too great. Neither reason is valid. If any incumbent, or anyone who has the responsibility for the care of hatchments which need attention, will write to me, I shall be happy to tell him how the hatchments may be simply and satisfactorily restored at a minimal cost. It is hoped that the publication of this survey will help to draw attention to the importance of these heraldic records.

The diamond-shaped hatchment, which originated in the Low Countries, is a debased form of the medieval achievement — the shield, helm, and other accoutrements carried at the funeral of a noble or knight. In this country it was customary for the hatchment to be hung outside the house during the period of mourning, and thereafter be placed in the church. This practice, begun in the early 17th century, is by no means entirely obsolete, for about 80 examples have so far been recorded for the present century.

Closely allied to the diamond hatchment, and contemporary with the earlier examples, are rectangular wooden panels bearing coats of arms. As some of these bear no inscriptions and a black/white or white/black background, and as some otherwise typical hatchments bear anything from initials and a date to a long inscription beginning 'Near here lies buried . . .', it will be appreciated that it is not always easy to draw a firm line between the true hatchment and the memorial panel. Any transitional types will therefore also be listed, but armorial boards which are clearly intended as simple memorials will receive only a brief note.

With hatchments the background is of unique significance, making it possible to tell at a glance whether it is for a bachelor or spinster, husband or wife, widower or widow. These different forms all appear on the plate immediately following this introduction.

Royal Arms can easily be mistaken for hatchments, especially in the West Country where they are frequently of diamond shape and with a black background. But such examples often bear a date, which proves that they were not intended as hatchments. Royal hatchments, however, do exist, and any examples known will be included.

All hatchments are in the parish church unless otherwise stated, but by no means are they all in churches; many are in secular buildings and these, if they have no links with the parish in which they are now found, are listed at the end of the text. All hatchments recorded since the survey began are listed, including those which are now missing.

Norfolk and Suffolk are both rich in hatchments. Norfolk I tackled myself with the aid of a number of competent helpers, whose work is duly acknowledged in the Introduction to that county. For Suffolk we are indebted to Miss Joan Corder, F.S.A. who, aided by photography and her unrivalled knowledge of the heraldry of the county, has produced a record which, for accuracy of blazon and genealogical detail, is a work of scholarship it would be hard to fault. I should like to join with her in acknowledging the work of Mr. Harold Hawes and Mr. E. K. Stephenson, with whom I corresponded for many years on the subject of Suffolk hatchments when the Survey began in 1952.

The illustrations on the following two pages are the work of the late Mr. G. A. Harrison and will provide a valuable 'key' for those unfamiliar with the complexity of hatchment backgrounds.

Peter G. Summers
Day's Cottage, North Stoke, Oxford

1.   MARRIED MAN

2.   MARRIED WOMAN

3.   BACHELOR

4.   WIDOW

5.   WIDOWER

6.   SPINSTER

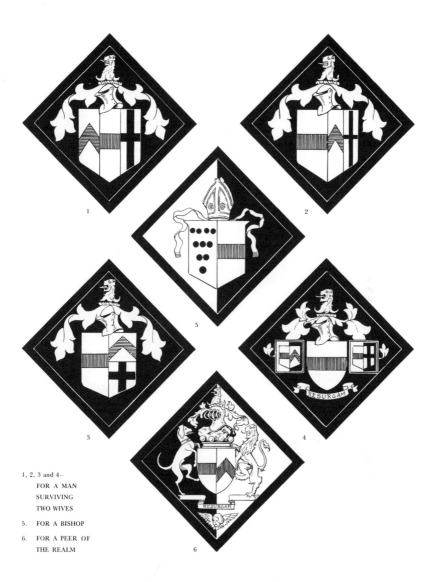

1, 2, 3 and 4—
  FOR A MAN
  SURVIVING
  TWO WIVES

5.   FOR A BISHOP

6.   FOR A PEER OF
  THE REALM

ABBREVIATIONS

B.P.	=	*Burke's Peerage, Baronetage and Knightage*
B.L.G.	=	*Burke's Landed Gentry*
B.E.P.	=	*Burke's Extinct and Dormant Peerages*
Copinger	=	W. A. Copinger, *The Manors of Suffolk* (1905-1911)
E.A. Misc.	=	*East Anglian Miscellany* (1901-1958)
E.A.N. & Q.	=	*The East Anglian, or Notes and Queries, etc.* (1864-1910)
Farrer	=	E. Farrer, *Church Heraldry of Norfolk*
Farrer MS.	=	E. Farrer, MS. Church Heraldry of Suffolk
Gage's 'Thingoe'	=	J. Gage, *The History and Antiquities of Suffolk, Thingoe Hundred* (1838)
Mills MS.	=	A. Mills, MS. Heraldic Monumental Remains
Proc. S.I.A.	=	*Proceedings of the Bury and West Suffolk Archaeological Institute and the Suffolk Institute of Archaeology* (1848-still published)
Suckling	=	A. Suckling, *The History and Antiquities of the County of Suffolk* (1846 and 1848)
Top. & Gen.	=	*Topographer and Genealogist*

NOTE

Blazons throughout are exactly as noted at the time of recording, not as they ought to be.

NORFOLK

by

Peter Summers, F.S.A.

Snettisham: For Henry Styleman, 1819

INTRODUCTION

There are at least 233 hatchments in Norfolk. Many of these were recorded by me and by a few friends at the time the survey was started in the early 1950s. It is regrettable that some of the hatchments then recorded are now missing or have been destroyed; but on the other hand many, such as those at Warham St. Mary, which were in a deplorable state when recorded in 1952, are now in excellent condition as a result of expert cleaning and restoration—mainly the work of Mr. Bryan Hall. The blazons of those recently missing or destroyed are included.

Only six 17th century hatchments appear to have survived, the earliest probably being (if correctly ascribed) for Robert Hartwell, at Alby. There are no less than seven 20th century examples, excluding the two royal hatchments at Sandringham, and six of these are later than 1950.

Rectangular armorial panels are scarce in the county. A few have been recorded but not included here as they appear to be simple memorials rather than hatchments. Also omitted are the four 'hatchments' at East Harling as they are not genuine examples.

The present list is probably not comprehensive as a thorough search has not been carried out. Any errors will be rectified and omissions included in a supplementary volume to be published when the general county survey has been completed. Any such information will therefore be appreciated and should be sent to me as General Editor.

During the past year I have relied much on assistance from Norfolk residents in checking blazons, supplying details of hatchments hitherto unrecorded, and providing necessary genealogical details. I am particularly grateful

to Mr. C. P. H. Wilson, who has been a regular and consider-
able source of essential information, and to Mr. J. Wortley,
Mr. N. P. Wood, Mr. H. Jaques and Mr. C. G. Alexander, who
have each personally checked and amended many hatchment
blazons. Without their help it would not have been possible
to get the work done so quickly. To these and to the many
others who have helped in this survey I extend my thanks
and good wishes.

Peter Summers

ALBY

1. All black background
Sable a stag's head cabossed between the attires a cross formy fitchy
argent (Hartwell), impaling, Argent on a chief vert a cross tau between
two molets or (Drury)
No crest or motto   Mantling: Gules and argent
A very small hatchment, c. 2ft. x 2ft. outside frame, 18in. x 18in.
inside
Probably for Robert Hartwell, Esq., of Northamptonshire, who m.
Anne, dau. of Sir William Drury, lord justice and governor of Ire-
land, brother of Sir Drue Drury of Riddlesworth, and d.   (B.E.B.)

ANMER

1. All black background
Azure a molet argent pierced gules (Coldham)   In pretence: Argent
on a bend engrailed sable three eagles displayed or (Houghton)
Crest: A griffin's head gules pierced through the neck with an arrow
proper
Mantling: Gules and argent   Motto: Citius aut serius
For John Coldham, who m. Rachel, dau. of the Rev. William
Houghton, and d. 4 Jan. 1754, aged 56.   (Farrer; B.L.G. 5th ed.)

2. Sinister background black
Qly, 1st and 4th, Coldham, 2nd and 3rd, Houghton (bend not en-
grailed), impaling, Gules three arrows point downwards or (Hales)
Crest and mantling: As 1.   Palm branches flanking base of shield
For Elizabeth Hales, who m. John Coldham, and d. 8 Mar. 1760.
(B.L.G. 5th ed.; M.I. in church)

3. All black background
Coldham arms only
Crest and mantling: As 1.   Motto: In coelo quies   Palm branches
flanking base of shield
Probably for James Coldham, Esq., d. 20 Oct. 1791.   (M.I. in church)

4. Dexter background black
Coldham, impaling, Gules a chevron between three boars' heads erased
argent (Wright)
Crest and mantling: As 1.   Motto: In coelo quies   Palm branches
flanking base of shield
For James Coldham, who m. 1783, Elizabeth, dau. of Walter
Wright, Esq., of Bury St. Edmunds, and d.   (B.L.G. 5th ed.)

5. All black background

Qly, as 2., impaling, Qly, 1st and 4th, Argent on a chevron between
in chief two roundels sable each charged with a martlet argent and in
base a roundel sable charged with a trefoil slipped argent three
mascles or (Pratt), 2nd and 3rd, Sable on a chevron between three
peewits' heads erased argent three annulets sable (Glyour)
Crest and mantling: As 1.   Motto: In coelo quies   Palm branches
flanking base of shield
For Henry Walter Coldham, who m. 1834, Maria, 2nd dau. of Edward
Roger Pratt, Esq., of Ryston, and d.   (Farrer; B.L.G. 5th ed.)

6. Dexter background black

Coldham   In pretence: Qly, 1st and 4th, Sable a chevron ermine be-
tween three millrinds argent, on a chief argent a lion passant gules
(Turner), 2nd and 3rd, Per pale sable and gules a lion passant guar-
dant or (Neale)
Crest and mantling: As 1.   Palm branches flanking base of shield
For Robert Hales, Patent Customer, and formerly collector of His
Majesty's Customs at the Port of King's Lynn, who d. 12 Sept. 1780,
aged 48.
(Identical arms appear on a floor slab in the South Chapel, inscribed
as above)

AYLSHAM

1. Dexter background black

Qly of six, 1st, Argent a lion rampant guardant gules (Jermy), 2nd,
Per pale or and vert a lion rampant gules (Bigod), 3rd, Azure a bend
between six martlets or (Mounteney), 4th, Argent three lions rampant
and a chief gules (Yelverton), 5th, Qly gules and argent (Cock), 6th,
Argent three picks sable (Chare), impaling, Gules three cross crosslets
in bend or (Wrench)
To dexter of main shield, Jermy, impaling, Qly, 1st and 4th, Argent
three bars and a canton gules (Fuller), 2nd and 3rd, Or fretty sable on a
chief azure three molets or ( )   To sinister of main shield,
Jermy   In pretence:Qly, 1st and 4th, Argent a stork sable beaked and
legged gules (Starkey), 2nd and 3rd, Azure a fess nebuly ermine
between three crescents argent (Weld)
Crest: A griffin wings elevated gules   Mantling: Gules and argent
Motto: Splendidum in signe virtus
For John Jermy of Bayfield, who m. 1st, Mary, dau. of Samuel Fuller,
and 2nd, Mary, dau. and heiress of the Rev. William Starkey, and
3rd, Mary, dau. and co-heiress of Sir Benjamin Wrench, and d. 25 Oct.
1744.   (Farrer)

BARNINGHAM TOWN

1. Sinister background black
Argent six fleurs-de-lys azure a chief indented or (Paston),
impaling, Gules a saltire engrailed between four horses'
heads couped or (Clarke)
Crest: A griffin sejant in its beak a serpent or
Mantling: Gules and argent   Motto: De mieux je pense en mieux
Supporters: Dexter, A bear proper collared and chained or   Sinister,
An ostrich argent
Frame decorated with skulls and crossbones
For Mary, dau. of John Clarke, of Bale, who m. Edward Paston, of
Barningham, and d.   (Farrer)

2. Dexter background black
Sable a crescent argent (Mott), impaling, Argent three wolves' heads
erased sable on a chief gules three cinquefoils argent (Cremer)
Crest: An estoile of eight points argent
Motto: I shall rise again
For Thomas Mott, who m. 1784, Frances, dau. of the Rev. Robert
Cremer, Vicar of Wymondham, and d. 1788.   (B.L.G. 2nd ed.)

BEDINGHAM

1. All black background
Per pale ermine and gules a double-headed eagle ducally crowned or
(Stone), impaling, Argent a fess wavy sable between three griffins'
heads erased gules (?Miller)
Crest: A demi-double-headed eagle per pale ermine and gules ducally
crowned and winged or   Mantling: Gules and argent
For Robert Stone, who m. Elizabeth ?Miller, and d. 6 Jan. 1829. She
d. 28 Nov. 1855, aged 83.   (Farrer)
(In view of the background perhaps used subsequently for widow)

BEESTON ST. LAWRENCE

1. Dexter background black
Ermine on a chief sable three crescents or, at fess point the Badge of
Ulster (Preston), impaling, Paly bendy gules and argent, on a chief
or three cinquefoils azure (Bagge)
Crest: A crescent or   Mantling: Gules and argent
Motto: Lucem spero clariorem
For Sir Thomas Hulton Preston, 1st Bt., who m. 2nd, Jane, dau. of
Thomas Bagge, of Stradsett Hall, and d. 21 Apr. 1823.   (B.P. 1939
ed.)

2. Sinister background black
Qly, 1st, Preston, 2nd, Argent a fess sable between three apples gules
leaved vert (Appleton), 3rd, Sable a bend and in sinister chief a leopard's
face or (Isaac), 4th, Qly gules and argent in the first quarter an annulet
or (Cock), impaling, Ermine an eagle displayed gules langued and armed
or (Bedingfeld)
Mantling: Gules and or   Motto: In coelo quies
Cherub's head above shield
For Henriette Elizabeth, dau. of John Bedingfeld, of Beeston St
Andrew, who m. the Rev. George Preston, Rector of Beeston, and d.
25 Apr. 1828. (Farrer)

BEESTON-NEXT-MILEHAM

1. All black background
Gules a saltire embattled between four crescents argent (Barnwell),
impaling, Argent three roses gules a chief gules (Sparrow)
Crest: A wolf's head erased argent gorged with a collar embattled gules,
the collar charged with three roundels argent and chained argent
Mantling: Gules and argent   Motto: Loyal au mort
For the Rev. Charles Barnwell, b. 1705, Rector of Beeston, who m.
1735, Catherine, dau. of Samuel Sparrow, of Lavenham, and d. 23 Apr.
1774. She d. 20 Apr. 1774. Hatchment probably commemorates both
husband and wife, as both were buried at Beeston, 29 Apr. 1774.
(B.L.G. 5th ed.)
(In very poor condition, the wolf's head being almost indistinguishable)

BLICKLING HALL

1. Sinister background black
Sable an estoile or between two flaunches ermine, in centre chief the
Badge of Ulster (Hobart)   In pretence, and impaling, Argent a
chevron engrailed between three escallops sable (Britiffe)
Motto: Auctor pretiosa facit   Supporters: Dexter, A stag attired
proper, collared fusilly and corded or   Sinister, A talbot proper
collared fusilly and corded or
For Judith, dau. of Robert Britiffe, of Baconsthorpe, who m. as his 1st
wife, Sir John Hobart, Bt. (later 1st Earl of Buckinghamshire) and d.
1727.   (B.P. 1949 ed.)

2. Dexter background black
Two circular shields   Dexter, within Order of the Bath, Hobart
Sinister, Ermine on a fess azure cotised sable three crescents or
(Bristowe)

Earl's coronet   Crest: A bull passant per pale sable and gules bezanty
armed and with a ring through his nose or   Mantle: Gules and ermine
Motto: As 1.   Supporters: As 1., but stag is attired or
For Sir John Hobart, Bt., cr. Earl of Buckinghamshire, 1746, who m.
1st, Judith, dau. of Robert Britiffe, of Baconsthorpe. She d. 1727.
He m. 2nd, Elizabeth, sister of Robert Bristowe, and d. 22 Sept. 1756.
She d. 12 Sept. 1762.   (B.P. 1949 ed.)

BRACON ASH

1. All black background (should be D. Bl.)
Per pale azure and gules a cross engrailed ermine (Berney)   Two escutcheons of pretence: Dexter, Per pale argent and azure on the dexter
three pallets sable, over all a bend or (Trench)   Sinister, two coats
per fess: Azure on a fess between three fleurs-de-lys argent three molets
gules (Dolens), Argent three roundels gules (Bayly)
Crest: From a duke's coronet or a plume of five feathers argent
Motto: Ascended
For John Berney, of Bracon Hall, who m. 1st, 1745, Susan, dau. and
sole heir of Samuel Trench, and 2nd, 1755, Margaret, dau. and heir of
Sir Daniel Dolens, and d. 18 Oct. 1800. She d. 4 Mar. 1801.
(B.L.G. 1914 ed.)

2. Dexter background black
Qly, 1st and 4th, Berney, 2nd and 3rd, Trench, impaling, Qly, 1st and
4th, Gules a fess between three swans argent (Jackson), 2nd and 3rd,
Azure a cross flory or (Ward)
Crest: From a duke's coronet or a plume of five feathers, one, three and
five argent, two and four azure   Motto: Resurgam
For Thomas Berney, of Bracon Hall, who m. 1774, Elizabeth, 3rd dau.
and co-heir of Sir George Jackson, Bt. and d. 21 Nov. 1786.
(B.L.G. 1914 ed.)

3. Identical to 2.
Except for motto, which is 'In coelo quies'

4. All black background
On a lozenge surmounted by a cherub's head
Arms: As 2.
Motto: Fidelis usque ad mortem
For Elizabeth, widow of Thomas Berney.   She d. 5 Jan. 1839,
(B.L.G. 1914 ed.)

5. Dexter backbround black
Qly of six, 1st, Berney, 2nd, Gules a chevron engrailed between three
garbs argent (Reedham), 3rd, Gules a chevron between three eagles

displayed argent (Caston), 4th, Argent on a canton gules a cross or
(Bradeston), 5th, Azure a bend ermine between six billets or (Smith),
6th, Trench, impaling, Per pale indented argent and gules in dexter
chief a wolf's head couped sable (Penrice)
Crest: As 1.   Mantling: Gules and or   Motto: In God is my trust
For Thomas Trench Berney, who m. 1812, Mary (d. 5 February 1876),
dau. of Thomas Penrice, of Gt. Yarmouth, and d. 15 Sept. 1869.
(B.L.G. 1914 ed.)

6. Dexter background black
Qly of six, 1st, Berney, 2nd, Reedham, 3rd, Smith, 4th, Trench, 5th,
Ward, 6th, Jackson, impaling. Per fess argent and ermine three battle-
axes sable (Gibbes)
Crest: From a ducal coronet or a plume of five feathers, one, three and
five azure, two and four gules.   Motto: In God is my trust
For Augustus Berney, who m. 1858, Matilda Lavinia, dau. of Col.
John George Nathaniel Gibbes, and d. 27 Sept. 1910.
(B.L.G. 1914 ed.)

BROOME

1. All black background except for sinister impalement
Qly of eleven, 1st and 11th, Or a chevron engrailed gules between three
cinquefoils sable, on a chief gules a lion passant argent (Cooke), 2nd,
Or a cross between four cocks gules (Cokerell), 3rd, Gules a crescent
between six martlets argent (Bohun), 4th, Sable nine fleurs-de-lys
three, three, three argent (Dallinhowe), 5th, Or a fess between three
crescents sable (   ), 6th, Argent on a fess between three griffins'
heads erased sable three fleurs-de-lys argent (   ), 7th, Or a fess
between three leopards' heads couped sable (   ), 8th, Sable a
chevron or between three fleurs-de-lys argent (   ), 9th, Sable a cross
or (Shelton), 10th, Ermine a chief indented gules (Brome), in fess
point the Badge of Ulster, impaling to dexter, Qly of nine, 1st and
9th, Sable a cinquefoil ermine a bordure engrailed or (Astley), 2nd, Or
a lion rampant gules crowned argent (Constable), 3rd, Sable crusilly a
cinquefoil pierced argent (Umfraville), 4th, Sable a cross engrailed or
(Charnell), 5th, Ermine on a bend sable three stags' heads cabossed
argent (   ), 6th, Sable a fess between two chevrons argent (   ),
7th, Gyronny of eight or and sable four martlets in cross counterchanged (Sybells), 8th, Gules on each of two chevrons argent three
crosses formy sable a bordure argent (Deane), and impaling to sinister,
Qly, 1st and 4th, Sable a chevron ermine between three saltires couped
argent (Greenwood), 2nd and 3rd, Or on a fess gules between three
trees proper three escallops argent (Greenwood)
Crest: A stag's head erased or attired gules   Mantling: Gules and
argent

For Sir William Cooke, 1st Bt., who m. 1st, Mary, dau. of Thomas Astley, of Melton Constable, and 2nd, Mary, relict of William Stuart of Wisbech, and dau. of William Greenwood of Burgh Castle, Suffolk, and d. 1681 or 1682. (Farrer; B.E.B.: 'Complete Baronetage'). (N.B.—This hatchment has been inaccurately repainted with the quarterings incorrectly marshalled. The blazon given above is as recorded in 1953 before restoration)

2. **All black background**
On a lozenge surmounted by a cherub's head
Cooke, with Badge of Ulster, impaling to dexter, Or a fess chequy argent and sable (Stuart), and to sinister, Greenwood
Winged hourglass below shield
Frame decorated with skulls and crossbones
For Mary, widow of Sir William Cooke, Bt. She d. 14 Feb. 1686.
(Farrer)

3. **Sinister background black**
Argent a chevron gules on a chief gules three molets or (Fowle), impaling, Or on a bend azure three leopards' faces argent (Mingay)
Crest: A griffin's head erased argent pierced through the neck with an arrow gules headed and feathered argent   Mantling: Gules and argent
Frame decorated with skulls and crossbones
For Anne (Mingay), 1st wife of John Fowle. She d. (Farrer)

4. **Sinister background black**
Argent a chevron gules on a chief gules three molets pierced argent (Fowle), impaling, two coats per pale, 1st, Mingay, 2nd, Gules on a fess argent between three crescents or three escallops sable (Ellis)
Crest and mantling: As 3.   Winged hourglass below shield
Frame decorated with skulls and crossbones
For Mary, dau. of Thomas Else, who m. as his second wife, John Fowle, and d. 6 Dec. 1722. (Farrer: M.I. in church)

5. **All black background**
Qly, 1st and 4th, Argent a chevron gules on a chief gules three molets or (Fowle), 2nd, Mingay, 3rd, Ellis
Crest and mantling: As 3.
Frame decorated with skulls, crossbones, sickles, hourglasses, etc.
Probably for John Fowle, husband of 3. and 4.   He d. 9 Nov. 1732.
(Farrer; M.I. in church)

6. **Dexter background black**
Argent a chevron gules on a chief gules three molets pierced argent (Fowle)
In pretence: Or on a chief sable two molets or (   )

Crest: As 3.
Unidentified

7. **Dexter background black**
Argent a chevron gules on a chief gules three molets or (Fowle)   In
pretence: Argent three tuns gules (   )
Crest: As 3.
Unidentified

BYLAUGH

1. **All black background**
Qly, 1st and 4th, Azure two weaving combs in fess between two broken
halves of a tilting spear in fess or (Lombe), 2nd and 3rd, Ermine a fess
engrailed or between three lions rampant proper (Hase), over all the
Badge of Ulster
Crest: Two tilting spears in saltire or pendent from each a forked pen-
non gules   Mantling: Gules and argent   Motto: Propositi tenax
For Sir John Lombe, 1st Bt., son of John Hase and Mary Lombe, d.
unm. 27 May 1817.   (Farrer; B.L.G. 1937 ed.)

CAISTER

1. **Dexter background black**
Vert three salmon hauriant argent (Salmon), impaling, Vert three bars
or over all a bend argent (   )
Crest: A dexter arm vambraced holding a cudgel proper
Mantling: Gules and argent
Motto: Resurgam   Skull below
Probably for William Orton Salmon, formerly of Bengal Civil Service.
His widow Elizabeth Frederica, d. 11 Apr. 1849.   (M.I. in church)

CATTON

1. **Dexter background black**
Argent a chevron sable between three Moors' heads proper (Ives)
In pretence: Azure a chevron argent between three chaplets vert
(? originally argent) flowered gules (Buckle)
Crest: A Moor's head proper   Mantling: Gules and argent
Motto: Resurgam
For Jeremiah Ives, of Catton and Norwich, Mayor 1786 and 1801,
who m. 1776, Frances, dau. and co-heir of Charles Buckle, of Norwich,
and d. 1820, aged 66.   (Campling's E. A. Pedigrees, p. 118)

2. All black background
On a lozenge   Arms: As 1.
For Frances, widow of Jeremiah Ives. She d. 1835.   (Source, as 1.)

EAST DEREHAM

1. Dexter background black
Lozengy gules and argent (Bagge), impaling, Sable a fess chequy azure
and or between eight billets argent (Lee)
Crest: A pair of wings addorsed argent charged with a cinquefoil azure
Mantling: Gules and argent   Motto: Resurgam
Two cherubs' heads above shield
For Charles Elsden Bagge, M.D. of Quebec House, who m. 1782, Anne,
only dau. and heir of Thomas Lee-Warner, and d. 29 Apr. 1799.
(B.L.G. 1937 ed.)
(This hatchment was recorded in 1955, but has since disappeared)

DICKLEBURGH

1. Dexter background black
Argent a bend between six storks sable (Starkie)   In pretence: Per
chevron or and azure, in chief two fleurs-de-lys gules, in base five
lozenges or each charged with an escallop gules (Edgar)
Crest: A stork sable   Mantling: Gules and argent
Motto: Mors janua vitae
For Nicholas Starkie, who m. Catherine Edgar, and d. 10 May 1797.
(Farrer;   Crisp's 'Visitations', 1906, Vol. 6)

2. All black background
Azure two bars or ermined sable, over all a bend countercompony or
ermined sable and gules (Lee), impaling, Argent a cross engrailed
between four roses gules (? Aiton)
Crest: A bear statant proper, muzzled, collared and chained argent, and
charged on the shoulder with a bezant   Mantling: Gules and argent
Motto: Resurgam
For George Lee, of Dickleburgh, and of Lombard Street, who d.
4 May 1828.   (Farrer)

DIDLINGTON

1. Dexter background black
Qly, 1st and 4th, Gules three tilting spears erect in fess or points argent
(Amherst), 2nd, Per saltire argent and or, in pale two dexter cubit arms
fesswise vested gules cuffed azure the hands proper each holding a

crosslet fitchy gules, in fess two lions rampant gules (Daniel), 3rd, Or
on a chevron azure between three French marigolds slipped and leaved
proper two lions passant respectant or, a bordure compony argent and
azure (Tyssen)   In pretence: Argent a fess between three moles
sable (Mitford)
Baron's coronet   Crests: 1. A cubit arm as above, surmounted by a
trefoil slipped vert 2. A tilting spear or headed argent in pale and surmounted by two others in saltire, encircled by a laurel wreath proper
3. A demi-lion rampant per fess or and azure, ducally crowned gules, in
its paws an escutcheon azure charged with an estoile or
Motto: Victoria concordia crescit
Supporters: Two herons proper collared or
Frame covered in black cloth
For William, 1st Baron Amherst of Hackney, who m. 1856, Susan, only
child of Admiral Robert Mitford, of Hunmanby Hall and Mitford
Castle, and d. 16 Jan. 1909.   (B.P. 1949 ed.)

2. **Dexter background black**
Or on a chevron azure between three French marigolds slipped and
leaved proper two lions passant respectant or (Tyssen)
Crest: A demi-lion rampant or ducally crowned gules in its paws an
escutcheon azure charged with an estoile or
Mantling: Gules and argent   Motto: Post mortem virtus virescit
Unidentified

DOWNHAM MARKET

1. **All black background**
Per pale azure and gules three chevrons argent each charged with
another couped and counterchanged (Say), impaling, Or three molets
sable (Ives)
Crest: A stag's head erased argent attired or   Mantling: Gules and
argent
Frame missing
For William Say, who m. Hannah, dau. of Thomas Ives of Watton, and
d. 16 Oct. 1751.   (M.I. in church)

2. **All black background**
On a lozenge surmounted by two cherubs' heads
Say, impaling, Sable a fess ermine between three bells argent (Bell)
Frame missing
For the widow of William Say (d. 14 Jan. 1775, aged 43). She d.
(M.I. in church)

EARLHAM

1. Dexter background black
Argent a cross engrailed gules (Gurney), impaling, Vert a bend cotised or (Pearse)
Crests: 1. On a chapeau gules and ermine a gurnard in pale head downwards proper 2. A wrestling collar or
For John Gurney, of Earlham Hall, who m. 1842, Laura Elizabeth, dau. and co-heir of the Rev. George Pearse, Vicar of Martham, and d. 23 Sept. 1856. (B.L.G. 1937 ed.)

EARSHAM

1. Dexter background black
Ermine on a bend sable three acorns or, the Badge of Ulster (Dalling)
In pretence: Or a chevron ermine between three lions passant gules (Lawford)
Crest: A cubit arm vested sable, cuffed argent, the hand grasping a sprig of oakleaves fructed proper Mantling: Gules and argent
Motto: Mors janua vitae
For General Sir John Dalling, 1st Bt., who m. Louisa, dau. of Exelbree Lawford, and d. 17 Jan. 1798. (Farrer)

2. All black background
On a lozenge surmounted by a cherub's head
Dalling (bend gules), with Badge of Ulster In pretence: Or a chevron sable ermined argent between three lions passant gules (Lawford)
Motto: In coelo quies
For Louisa, widow of Sir John Dalling, 1st, Bt. She d. 28 Mar. 1824. (Farrer)

3. Black black background
Dalling arms only, as 1., with Badge of Ulster
Crest: A cubit arm vested argent the hand grasping a sprig of oak leaves fructed proper Mantling: Gules and argent Motto: Resurgam
For Sir William Dalling, 2nd Bt., of Earsham Hall, who d. 16 Feb. 1864. (Farrer)

ELLINGHAM

1. Dexter background black
Per bend indented or and azure two crosses moline pierced and counterchanged (Smith), impaling, Gules a fess between three eagles wings expanded or (Johnson)
Crest: From a ducal coronet or a dove wings expanded argent

Mantling: Gules and argent   Motto: Resurgam
For Henry Smith, of Ellingham Hall, who m. Maria, dau. of the Rev.
William Johnson, and d.   (Farrer)

2. **All black background**
On a lozenge   Argent a chevron ermine between three chamber
pieces sable firing proper (Chambers), impaling, Sable an estoile or
between two flaunches ermine (Hobart)
A very small hatchment, c. 12in. x 12in., on a wood panel
Unidentified

NORTH ELMHAM

1. **Dexter background black**
Ermine a millrind between two martlets in pale sable, on a chief
engrailed azure two marlions wings conjoined or (Milles), impaling,
Azure three cross crosslets fitchy in bend between two bendlets or
(Knatchull)
Baron's coronet   Crest: A lion rampant or ermined sable holding
between the paws a millrind sable   Motto: Esto quod esse videris
Supporters: Dexter, A griffin argent ducally gorged or   Sinister, A
bear proper collared with a belt, buckled, the strap pendent argent
charged with two crescents or, the buckles and edges or
For George John, 4th Baron Sondes, who m. 1823, Eleanor, dau. of
Sir Edward Knatchbull, 8th Bt., and d. 10 Sept. 1894.   (B.P. 1949
ed.)
(There is an identical hatchment in the parish church of Sheldwich,
Kent)

ELSING HALL

1. **Dexter background black**
Sable three lions passant in bend between two bendlets argent (Browne)
In pretence: Qly gules and azure a cross ermine (Berney)
Crest: An eagle displayed vert   Mantling: Gules and argent
Motto: Suivez raison
For the Rev. Richard Browne, who m. 1786, Frances, only dau. and
heiress of Thomas Berney, of Kings Lynn, and d. 11 May 1821.
(B.L.G. 5th ed.)

2. **All black background**
On a lozenge surmounted by two cherubs' heads
Azure three bucks trippant or (Greene)   In pretence: Browne
Motto: Resurgam

For Mary, only dau. and heiress of Thomas Browne, who m. 1770,
Thomas Green of Marlingford, and d. 10 June 1798.   (Farrer)

FELBRIGG

1. Dexter background black
Azure a chevron between three lions' heads erased or (Windham),
impaling, Gules a fess wavy between three fleurs-de-lys or (Hicks)
Crest: A lion's head erased within a fetterlock or
Mantling: Gules and argent.   Motto: In coelo quies
For Col. William Windham, who m. Sarah (née Hicks), widow of
Robert Lukin, and d. 30 Oct. 1762.   (Farrer)

2. All black background
On a lozenge surmounted by a cherub's head
Windham, impaling, Argent on a mount vert three trees proper
(Forrest)
Motto: In coelo quies
For Cecilia Frederica, dau. of Commodore Arthur Forrest, who m. the
Rt. Hon. William Windham, and d. 5 May 1824.   (M.I. in church)

3. Dexter background black
Windham, impaling, Qly, 1st and 4th, Gules two dexter wings in pale
argent each charged with two trefoils sable, 2nd and 3rd, Or a tree
eradicated proper, pendent from it a shield gules charged with three
escallops argent (Thellusson)
Crest and mantling: As 1.   Motto: Abstulit qui dedit
Skull below shield
For Vice-Admiral William Windham, who m. 1801, Anne, dau. of
Peter Thellusson, of Broadsworth, Yorks, and d. 12 Jan. 1833.
(Farrer; B.L.G. 2nd ed.)

4. Dexter background black
Windham, impaling, Gules on a bend argent three trefoils slipped vert
(Hervey)
Crest: As 1.   Mantling: Azure and or   Motto: Au bon droit
For William Howe Windham, who m. 1835, Sophia, dau. of Frederick
William, 1st Marquess of Bristol, and d. 22 Dec. 1854.   (Farrer)

GARBOLDISHAM

1. All black background
Qly, 1st and 4th, qly. i. and iv. Azure a branch of palm tree in bend
sinister between three fleurs-de-lys or (Montgomerie), ii. and iii.
Gules three rings argent (Eglinton), 2nd, Qly azure and or a cross flory

counterchanged (Molineux), 3rd, Per pale argent and sable on a chevron five horseshoes counterchanged (Crisp)
To dexter of main shield, Qly, as main shield, impaling, ?   S.Bl.
To sinister of main shield, Qly, as main shield, impaling, Argent a fess engrailed between three cinquefoils sable (Foley)   D.Bl.
Crests: Two, both indistinguishable   Mantling: Azure and or
Motto: Resurgam
For Thomas Molineux-Montgomerie, of Garboldisham Hall, who m. 1st, Marianne Robarts (d.s.p. 1842), and 2nd, Georgiana, dau. of Thomas, 3rd Lord Foley, and d. 28 Feb. 1855.   She d. Nov. 1864. (B.L.G, 1937 ed.)
(The hatchment is very dirty and no further details can be ascertained without cleaning)

GUESTWICK

1. Sinister background black (should be D.Bl.)
Qly, 1st and 4th, Gules on a chevron argent between three eagles reguardant or three cinquefoils sable (Bulwer), 2nd and 3rd, Or three molets azure, on a chief wavy azure a dove reguardant argent (Wiggett)
In pretence: Azure a fess double cotised or (Earle)
Crest: A goat's head ermine   Mantling: Gules and argent
Motto: In adversis major par secundis
Skull below shield
For William Wiggett Bulwer, of Wood Dalling, who m. 1756, Mary, eldest dau. of Augustine Earle, of Heydon, and d. 5 Apr. 1793.
(B.L.G. 1937 ed.: Farrer)

2. All black background
On a lozenge   Bulwer   In pretence: Earle
For Mary, widow of William Wiggett Bulwer.   She d. 12 Feb. 1798.
(Farrer)

3. Dexter background
Qly of eight, 1st and 8th, Bulwer, 2nd, Wiggett (chief not wavy), 3rd, Earle, 4th, Argent three castles sable (Castell), 5th, Gyronny argent and azure on a saltire gules an annulet argent (Gage), 6th, Gules a cross flory argent between four lions' heads erased or (Beck), 7th, Argent on a bend sable three wolves' heads erased or within a bordure engrailed or (Yonge), impaling, Ermine on a chief azure three crowns or (Lytton)
Crest: A goat's head proper   Mantling: Or and argent
Motto: (In) adversis major par secundus   Skull and crossbones below shield
For William Earle Bulwer, of Heydon Hall, who m. 1798, Elizabeth Barbara, dau. and sole heir of Richard Warburton Lytton, of Knebworth Park, Herts, and d. 7 July 1807.   (B.L.G. 1937 ed.; Farrer)

(The hatchment of Elizabeth Barbara, widow of William Earle Bulwer, is in the parish church of Knebworth, Herts)

GUNTON

1. **Dexter background black**
Qly, 1st and 4th, Qly azure and gules an imperial crown or between four lions rampant argent (Harbord), 2nd and 3rd, Argent on a chief gules three owls argent (Cropley), impaling, Gules three cross crosslets in bend or (Wrench)   To dexter of main sheld, Qly as main shield, in pretence, Ermine on a fess sable three lions rampant or (Rant), also impaling Rant.   A.Bl.   To sinister of main shield, Arms as main shield D.Bl.
Crest: On a chapeau gules and ermine a lion couchant argent langued gules
Mantling: Gules and argent   Motto: Aequanimitur
For Harbord Harbord, who m. 1st, Jane, dau. of Sir William Rant. She d. 21 Oct. 1735.   He m. 2nd, – Wrench, and d. 6 Feb. 1741.
(Mon. in church)

2. **Dexter background black**
Qly, 1st and 4th, Harbord, 2nd, qly i. and iv. Argent a chevron engrailed between three escallops sable (Britiffe), ii. and iii. Rant, 3rd, Argent a fleur-de-lys gules (Morden), in centre chief the Badge of Ulster   In pretence: Argent a pierced molet sable (Assheton)
Baron's coronet   Crest and motto: As 1.   Mantle: Gules and ermine   Supporters: Dexter, A lion or collared and chained azure Sinister, A leopard guardant collared and chained or
For Harbord, 1st Baron Suffield, who m. 1760, Mary, dau. and co-heiress of Sir Ralph Assheton, Bt., and d. 4 Feb. 1810.
(B.P. 1949 ed.)

3. **Dexter background black**
Qly, 1st and 4th, Harbord, 2nd and 3rd, Morden   In pretence: Qly, 1st and 4th, Sable an estoile or between two flaunches ermine (Hobart), 2nd and 3rd, Argent on a chief vert a cross tau between two molets or (Drury)
Baron's coronet   Crest, mantle and motto: As 2.   Supporters: Dexter, A lion or ducally gorged and chained azure   Sinister, A talbot reguardant proper, collared fusilly and corded or
For William Assheton, 2nd Baron Suffield, who m. 1792, Caroline, dau. of John, 2nd Earl of Buckinghamshire, and d.s.p. 1 Aug. 1821.
(B.P. 1949 ed.)

4. Dexter background black
Qly of nine, 1st, Harbord, 2nd, Morden, 3rd, Cropley (owls on pile),
4th, Britiffe, 5th, covered by inescutcheon, 6th, Assheton, 7th, Ermine
on a fess gules three annulets or (Barton), 8th, Paly of six argent and
vert (   ), 9th, Argent a cross moline sable (   ), in centre chief
the Badge of Ulster   In pretence, Qly, 1st and 4th, Azure two bars
argent (Venables), 2nd, Argent a fret sable (Vernon), 3rd, Or on a fess
azure three garbs or (Vernon), also impaling, Qly, 1st, Paly of six or
and azure a canton ermine (Shirley), 2nd, Argent a fess and in chief
three roundels gules (Devereux), 3rd, Argent a cross engrailed gules
between four water bougets sable (Bourchier), 4th, Qly France and
England within a bordure argent (Plantagenet)
Baron's coronet   Crest and motto: As 1.   Supporters: Dexter, A
lion or ducally gorged and chained azure   Sinister, A leopard
guardant proper ducally gorged and chained or langued gules
For Edward, 3rd Baron Suffield, who m. 1st, 1809, Georgiana, dau. and
heiress of George, 2nd Lord Vernon, and 2nd, Emily Harriot, dau. of
Evelyn Shirley, of Ettington Park, Warwick, and d. July 1835.
(B.P. 1949 ed.)

5. Dexter background black
Qly. of nine, as 4., impaling, Or on a chevron gules between three
griffins' heads erased azure an anchor erect between two lions passant
combatant or   (Gardner)
Baron's coronet   Crest and motto: As 1.   Supporters: As 4.
For Edward Vernon, 4th Baron Suffield, who m. 1835, Charlotte
Susannah, only dau. of Alan, 2nd Baron Gardner, and d.s.p. 22 Aug.
1853.   (B.P. 1949 ed.)

WEST HARLING

1. Dexter background black
Qly, 1st and 4th, Argent on a chevron gules between three buglehorns
sable three molets pierced or (Colborne), 2nd and 3rd, Gules on a
chevron between three doves argent three roundels sable (Ridley),
impaling, Argent a bend paly of six ermine and sable between two
lions' heads erased gules, on a chief azure three billets argent (Steele)
Baron's coronet   Crests: Dexter, A stag's head proper ducally collared or, pendent therefrom a buglehorn sable   Sinister, A bull
passant gules
Supporters: Dexter, A bull gules on his shoulder three molets pierced or
Sinister, A stag proper ducally collared or, pendent therefrom a buglehorn sable   Motto: Constans fidei
For Nicholas, 1st Baron Colborne, who m. 1808, Charlotte, dau. of the
Rt. Hon. Thomas Steele, and d. 3 May 1854.   (B.P. 1949 ed.)

HEACHAM

1. Dexter background black
Sable a unicorn passant or on a chief or three billets sable (Styleman),
impaling, Per chevron gules and sable in chief two swans respectant
argent in base a herring proper (Cobb)
Crest: A greyhound's head erased proper collared and corded or
Mantling: Gules and argent   Motto: In coelo quies
For Nicholas Styleman, who. m. Elizabeth, dau. of Frank Cobb, of
Margate, and d. 30 Apr. 1830.   (B.L.G. 2nd ed.; M.I. in church)

2. All black background
On a lozenge   Arms: As 1.
Mantling: Gules and argent   Motto: Resurgam
For Elizabeth, widow of Nicholas Styleman.   She d. 27 Jan. 1831.
(Sources, as 1.)

3. Dexter background black
Gyronny of eight azure and or on a chief gules three annulets or
(Rolfe)
In pretence: Qly, 1st, Per pale vert and gules a fleur-de-lys argent
(Folkes), 2nd, Ermine on a fess indented sable a ducal coronet or
between two escallops argent (Taylor), 3rd, Argent a fess chequy or
and azure (Steward), 4th, Sable a crescent argent (Hovell)
Crest: A garb or   Mantling: Gules and argent
Motto: Mors janua vitae
For Edmund Rolfe, who m. 1764, Dorothy, dau. of William Folkes, of
Hillington Hall, and d. 7 Mar. 1817.   (Sources, as 1.)

4. All black background
On a lozenge   Arms: As 3.
Motto: In coelo quies
For Dorothy, widow of Edmund Rolfe.   She d. 21 Mar. 1829.
(Sources, as 1.)

5. Dexter background black
Qly, 1st and 4th, Rolfe, 2nd, Folkes, 3rd, Taylor, impaling, Argent
three greyhounds courant in pale sable (Biscoe)
Crest and mantling: As 3.   Motto: Resurgam
For Edmund Rolfe, who m. Catherine Frances, dau. of Elisha Biscoe of
Spring Gardens, Middlesex, and d.s.p. 17 Dec. 1836.   (Sources, as 1.)

6. All black background
On a lozenge   Arms: As 5.
Mantling: Gules and argent   Motto: Resurgam
For Catherine Frances, widow of Edmund Rolfe.   She d. 26 Jan. 1837.
(Sources, as 1.)

HETHEL

1. Sinister background black
Argent a chevron between three griffins passant sable (Finch), impaling,
Per pale or and argent on a chief indented sable three lions rampant or
(Beevor)
Crest: A griffin passant sable   Mantling: Gules and argent
Motto: Mors janua vitae
Frame decorated with skulls and crossbones
For Anna Bettina, dau. of Thomas Beevor, who m. William Finch
Finch, of Shelford, Cambs., and d. 3 Feb. 1780.   (Farrer)

2. Sinister background black
Qly, 1st and 4th, Beevor, with Badge of Ulster in 1st qr., 2nd and 3rd,
Argent a fess sable between three bats displayed proper (Batt)   In
pretence: Qly, 1st, Or two bends engrailed sable (Branthwayt), 2nd,
Argent on a fess between three escutcheons gules three molets pierced
argent (Bacon), 3rd, Sable two shin bones in saltire argent (Newton),
4th, Azure on a chevron between three annulets argent three cinque-
foils azure (Tawell)
Motto: Suaviter in modo fortiter in re
For Elizabeth, dau. and heir of Miles Branthwayt, of Hethel, who m.
Sir Thomas Beevor, 1st Bt. and d. 15 Jan. 1794.   (B.P. 1949 ed.)

3. All black background
Arms: As 2, but with Badge of Ulster in 1st and 4th qrs.
Crest: A beaver passant sable
Motto: As 2.
For Sir Thomas Beevor, 1st Bt., who m. Elizabeth, dau. and heir of
Miles Branthwayt, of Hethel, and d. 18 Feb. 1814.   (B.P. 1949 ed.)

4. Dexter background black
Qly of eight, 1st and 6th, with Badge of Ulster on 1st qr., 2nd and 5th,
Batt, 3rd, Branthwayt, 4th, Bacon, 7th, Newton, 8th, Tawell, with
field gules and five cinquefoils   In pretence: Gules two bars and a
chief indented or (Hare)
Crest: A beaver passant proper   Mantling: Gules and argent
Motto: As 2.   Skull below shield
For Sir Thomas Beevor, 2nd Bt., who m. 1795, Anne, dau. and heir of
Hugh Hare, of Hargham Hall, and d. 10 Dec. 1820.   (B.P. 1949 ed.)

HEYDON

1. All black background
Sable a chevron engrailed ermine between three annulets argent (Davy),
impaling, Chequy or and sable a fess ermine (Calthorpe)

Crest: From a ducal coronet or a boar's head erased sable armed and chained or   Mantling: Gules and argent

For John Davy, of Heigham, who m. Judith Calthorpe, and d. 30 Jan. 1710.   (Farrer)

2. Sinister background black

Gules on a chevron argent between three eagles reguardant or three cinquefoils sable (Bulwer), impaling, Argent on a pale sable a demi-lucy couped or (Gascoyne)   Mantling: Gules and argent   Cherub's head above shield, skull and crossbones below

For Emily, dau. of General Isaac Gascoyne, who m. William Earle Lytton Bulwer of Heydon Hall, and d. 29 Dec. 1846.   (B.L.G. 1937 ed.)

3. Dexter background black

Two shields   Dexter, within the Order of the Bath, Gules on a chevron argent between three eagles reguardant or three cinquefoils sable (Bulwer) Sinister, within ornamental wreath, Bulwer, impaling, Qly, 1st and 4th, Gules a cross between twenty roundels argent (Wellesley), 2nd and 3rd, Or a lion rampant gules (Cowley)

Baron's coronet   Crests: Dexter, An antelope's head erased ermine, armed and maned or   Sinister, A dove reguardant holding an olive branch in its beak proper   Motto: Adversis major par secundis

Supporters: Dexter, A dragon vert, maned and armed gules semy of lozenges or Sinister, A lion rampant reguardant or collared gules pendent therefrom an escutcheon argent charged with a boar's head couped sable

For Henry Lytton, Baron Dalling and Bulwer, who m. 1848, Georgiana Charlotte Mary, dau. of Henry, 1st Baron Cowley, and d.s.p. 23 May 1872.   (B.P. 1949 ed.)

4. Dexter background black (extending behind main coat)

Qly, 1st and 4th, Bulwer, 2nd, Or three molets azure pierced gules, on a chief wavy sable a dove reguardant proper (Wiggett), 3rd, Ermine on a chief indented azure three ducal coronets or (Lytton), impaling, to the dexter, Argent on a pale sable a demi-lucy couped or (Gascoyne), and to the sinister, Argent on a cross engrailed gules five crescents or, on a chief azure three bezants (Green)

Crests and motto: As 3.

Mantling: Gules and argent

For William Earle Lytton Bulwer, who m. 1st, 1827, Emily, dau. of Gen. Isaac Gascoyne, and 2nd, 1841, Elizabeth, dau. of William Green, of Forty Hill, Enfield, and d. 21 July 1877.   (B.P. 1949 ed.)

(Hatchments 2, 3 and 4 are in the Bulwer mausoleum)

HOCKERING

1. Dexter background black
Gules a rose argent barbed and seeded proper, a chief ermine (Howman),
impaling, Azure on a chevron or between three martlets argent three
trefoils azure (? Wood)
Crest: On a mount vert a pegasus salient sable
Mantling: Gules and argent   Motto: Resurgam
Unidentified

HONING

1. Dexter background black
Sable a bow and arrow argent (Cubitt), impaling, Cubitt
Crest: A dexter arm embowed in armour with gauntlet holding an
arrow or tipped and feathered sable   Mantling: Gules and argent
Motto: Resurgam
For Edward George Cubitt, of Honing Hall, who m. 1859, Emma, dau.
of the Rev. Benjamin Lucas Cubitt, Rector of Catfield, and d. 20 Dec.
1865.   (B.L.G. 1937 ed.)

2. Dexter background black
Cubitt, impaling, Qly argent and gules, in the 2nd and 3rd qrs a fret or,
over all on a bend sable three escallops argent (Spencer)
Crest and mantling: As 1.
For Thomas Cubitt, of Honing Hall, who m. 1784, Catharine, dau. of
Henry Spencer, of Dulwich, and d. 19 Dec. 1829.   (B.L.G. 1937 ed.)

HONINGHAM

1. All black background
Qly, 1st and 4th, qly i. and iv. Sable a chevron ermine between three
escallops argent (Townshend), ii. and iii. Qly gules and or in the first
quarter a molet or, a crescent for difference (Vere), 2nd and 3rd,
Sable three swords in pile argent hilted or (Powlett)
Baron's coronet   Crest: A stag proper attired or
Mantling: Gules and ermine   Motto: Resurgam   No supporters
For Henry, 3rd Baron Bayning, Vicar of Honingham, who m. 1842,
Emma, only dau. of W. H. Fellowes, of Ramsey Abbey, Hunts, and d.
5 Aug. 1866.   (B.P. 1949 ed.)

HOUGHTON

1. **Dexter background black**
Or on a fess between two chevrons sable three cross crosslets or
(Walpole)
In pretence: Or on a fess dancetty between three billets urdy at the
foot azure each charged with a lion rampant or three bezants (Rolle)
The shield surrounded with the collar of the Order of the Bath
Earl's coronet   Crest: The bust of a man in profile couped proper
ducally crowned or, from the coronet a long cap gules charged with a
catherine wheel or   Mantling: Gules and ermine
Motto: Fari quae sentiat   Supporters: Dexter, An antelope argent
Sinister, A stag argent, attired proper, both collared counter-compony
or and azure chained or
For Robert, 2nd Earl of Orford, who m. 1724, Margaret, dau. and heir
of Samuel Rolle, of Haynton, Devon, and d. 1 Apr. 1751.
(B.P. 1878 ed.)

2. **All black background**
Walpole arms only
Earl's coronet   Crest, motto and supporters: As 1.
Mantle: Gules and ermine
Probably for George, 3rd Earl of Orford, who d. unm. 5 Dec. 1791
(B.P. 1878 ed.)

3. **and 4. Exactly as 2.**
One probably for Horace, 4th Earl of Orford, who d. unm. 5 Dec. 1791.
(B.P. 1878 ed.)
(There is an identical hatchment in the parish church at Wickmere)

5. **Dexter background**
Gules in chief two helmets in profile argent and in base a garb or
(Cholmondeley)   In pretence: Argent three battering rams fesswise
in pale or headed azure (Bertie)   The shield within the Order of the
Garter
Marquess's coronet   Crest: A demi-griffin sable armed and winged or
holding in its claws a helmet argent   Mantle: Gules and ermine
Motto: Cassis tutissima virtus   Supporters: Dexter, A griffin sable
armed and winged or   Sinister, A monk habited in grey with a staff
in his left hand proper
For George James, 1st Marquess of Cholmondeley, who m. 1791,
Georgiana Charlotte, dau. of Peregrine, 3rd Duke of Ancaster, and
d. 10 Apr. 1827.   (B.P. 1878 ed.)
(There is an identical hatchment at Cholmondeley Castle, and in the
parish church of Malpas, Cheshire)

6. All black background
On a lozenge   Qly, 1st and 4th, Cholmondeley, 2nd, Gules a chevron
between three griffins' heads erased argent (Edwardes), 3rd, Walpole
In pretence: Bertie
Marchioness's coronet   Supporters: As 5.
For Georgiana Charlotte, widow of George James, 1st Marquess of
Cholmondeley.   She d. 23 June 1838.   (B.P. 1878 ed.)
(There is an identical hatchment at Cholmondeley Castle, Cheshire)

7. Dexter background black
Cholmondeley, impaling, Qly France and England within a bordure
compony argent and azure (Somerset)
Marquess's coronet   Crest, mantling and motto: As 5.   Supporters
Dexter, as 5.   Sinister, A wolf argent collared azure
For George, 2nd Marquess of Cholmondeley, who m. 2nd, Susan, dau.
of Henry Charles, 6th Duke of Beaufort, and d.s.p. 8 May 1870.
(B.P. 1878 ed.)
(There is an identical hatchment at Cholmondeley Castle, and in the
parish church at Malpas, Cheshire)

8. Sinister background black
Cholmondeley, impaling, Azure a crescent between three molets argent
(Arbuthnot)
Marchioness's coronet   Supporters: Dexter, as 5.   Sinister, A wolf
or collared vair
For Marcia Emma Georgiana, dau. of the Rt. Hon. Charles Arbuthnot,
who m. William Henry Hugh, 3rd Marquess of Cholmondeley, and d.
3 Nov. 1878.   (B.P. 1949 ed.)

9. All black background
Cholmondeley, impaling, Qly, 1st and 4th, Arbuthnot, 2nd and 3rd
qly i. and iv. Argent a fess between two chevrons azure (   ), ii.
and iii.   Azure on a chevron between three storks argent three fleurs-
de-lys azure (   )
Marquess's coronet   Crest, mantling and motto: As 5.   Supporters: As 8.
For William Henry Hugh, 3rd Marquess of Cholmondeley, who d.
16 Dec. 1884.   (B.P. 1949 ed.)
(There is an identical hatchment at Cholmondeley Castle, Cheshire)

10. All black background
Cholmondeley   In pretence: Or a palm tree eradicated proper between on the dexter a pomegranate proper and on the sinister a branch
of laurel proper, on a chief azure a lion passant in the dexter paw a rod
erect or   (Sassoon)

Crest and motto: As 5.   Mantling: Gules and argent   Supporters:
As 8.   Behind the shield are two wands azure, for Lord High Chamberlain, and beneath the motto is a key or tied with a ribbon azure
For George Horatio Charles, 5th Marquess of Cholmondeley, who
m. 1913, Sybil Rachel Betty Cecile, dau. of Sir Edward Albert Sassoon,
2nd Bt., and d. 16 Sept. 1968.   (B.P. 1970 ed.)
The artist's initials and date, N M '69, are inscribed beneath the shield,
(This hatchment was painted by Norman Manwaring, who also painted
an identical hatchment at Cholmondeley Castle, Cheshire)

HOVETON ST. JOHN

1. **All black background**
Sable a chevron argent between three trefoils slipped or (Blofeld),
impaling, Ermine on a chief nebuly azure three escallops or (Negrus)
Crest: Three feathers, the centre azure, the outer argent
No mantling or motto
For Thomas Blofeld, who m. Sarah, dau. of Henry Negus of Hoveton
St. Peter, and d. 25 Dec. 1766.   (B.L.G. 1937 ed.; M.I. in church)

2. **Dexter background black**
Blofeld   In pretence: Blofeld
Crest: As 1.   Mantling: Vert and argent   Motto: Resurgam
For John Blofeld, who m. Sarah, only child of Thomas Blofeld, and d.
25 Aug. 1805.   (B.L.G. 1937 ed.)

3. **Dexter background black**
Qly, 1st and 4th, Blofeld, 2nd and 3rd, Blofeld, impaling, Qly argent
and gules, in the second and third quarters a fret or, over all on a bend
sable three escallops argent (Spencer)
Crest, mantling and motto: As 2.
For Thomas Blofeld, who m. Mary, dau. of Henry Spencer of Dulwich,
and d. 7 Aug. 1817.   (B.L.G. 1937 ed.;   Farrer)

4. **Sinister background black**
Qly, 1st and 4th, Blofeld, 2nd, Chequy or and azure a fess ermine
(Calthorpe), 3rd, Ermine a maunch gules (Calthorpe)   In pretence:
Or a Paschal Lamb proper on a mount vert bearing a banner, ermine a
cross gules (Grose)
Mantling: Gules and argent   Motto: Resurgam   Cherub's head
above shield
For Mary Caroline, dau. and heir of Francis Grose, who m. the Rev.
Thomas Calthorpe Blofeld, and d. 5 Jan. 1852.   (B.L.G. 1937 ed.)

5. All black background
Arms: As 4.
Crest, mantling and motto: As 2.
For the Rev. Thomas Calthorpe Blofeld, d. 1855.   (B.L.G. 1937 ed.)

HOVETON ST. PETER

1. Sinister background black
Sable a chevron between in chief two bunches of grapes and in base a
wolf rampant or (Aufrere), impaling, Sable on a chevron between three
roundels argent each charged with a martlet sable three mascles sable
(Pratt)
Shield surmounted by a skull
For Mary (Pratt), wife of Anthony Aufrere.   She d. 19 Feb. 1750.
(M.I. in church)

2. Dexter background black
Aufrere, impaling, Qly argent and gules, on the 2nd and 3rd quarters a
fret or, over all a fess azure (Norris)
Crest: A lion rampant or   Mantling: Gules and argent
For Anthony Aufrere, who m. 1756, Anne, dau. of John Norris, of
Witchingham, and d. 11 Sept. 1814.   (B.L.G. 5th ed.)

3. All black background
Arms: As 2.
Crest, mantling and motto: As 2
Presumably for Anne, widow of Anthony Aufrere (arms should be on
lozenge and without crest).   She d. 11 Apr. 1816.   (B.L.G. 5th ed.)

4. Dexter background
Ermine on a chief nebuly azure three escallops or, a crescent for differ-
ence (Negus), impaling, Argent a chevron gules, on a chief gules three
molets pierced argent (Fowle)
Crest: A dove or resting its dexter claw on an escallop azure
Mantling: Gules and argent
For Henry Negus, who m. 1683, Sarah, dau. of John Fowle, of Norwich.
and d. 1706.   (Rye's 'Norfolk Families'; Campling's 'E. Anglian
Pedigrees')

5. Dexter background black
Ermine on a chief nebuly azure three escallops or (Negus), impaling,
Sable a lion rampant argent (Palgrave)
Crest: A dove argent resting its dexter claw on an escallop or
Mantling: Gules and argent
For Henry Negus, of Hoveton, who m. Christian, dau. of Thomas
Palgrave, M.P. for Norwich, and d. 11 Apr. 1727.
(Sources, as 4.)

6. Sinister background black
Negus   In pretence: Argent a saltire sable on a chief gules two wool-
packs or (Johnson)
Crest: As 4.
For Christabella Johnson, of Carlisle, who m. as his 1st wife, Henry
Negus, High Sheriff in 1740, and d.   (Sources, as 4.)

7. Dexter background black
Negus, impaling, Per pale argent and gules on a fess engrailed or
between three greyhounds counterchanged a fleur-de-lys between two
lozenges gules   (White)
Crest and mantling: As 5.
For Henry Negus, who m. 1st, Christabella Johnson, and 2nd, 1780,
Hester White, and d. 1794.   (Sources, as 4.)

8. Sinister background black
Qly, 1st and 4th, Negus, 2nd and 3rd, Johnson   In pretence: Or on a
chief indented azure two molets pierced or (D'Eye)
Crest: As 5.
For Mary, dau. and co-heiress of Thomas D'Eye of Eye, who m. 1761,
Henry Negus, of Bungay, attorney, and d.   (Sources, as 4.)

9. All black background
Arms: As 8.
Crest: As 5.   Motto: Resurgam
For Henry Negus, of Bungay, attorney, who d.   (Sources, as 4.)

KETTERINGHAM

1. Sinister background black
Gules three martlets between two chevronels argent (Peach)   In
pretence: Argent a cross cotised of demi-fleurs-de-lys between four
molets pierced sable (Atkyns)
Crest: A lion rampant per fess ermine and gules ducally crowned or
Mantling: Gules and argent   Motto: In coelo quies
For Harriet, dau. of Thomas Atkyns, who m. Nathaniel William Peach,
and d. 3 July 1825.   (Farrer)

2. All black background
Arms: As 1.
Crest and mantling: As 1.   Motto: Resurgam
For Nathaniel William Peach, who d.   (Farrer)

3. All black background
Qly, 1st and 4th, Azure a castle triple-towered and in base a crescent or
(Boileau), 2nd and 3rd, Azure on a bend cotised or between six mascles

argent five escallops sable (Pollen), over all the Badge of Ulster, impaling, Qly, 1st and 4th, qly, i. and iv. Azure a chevron argent between three fleurs-de-lys or (Kynynmound), ii. and iii. Argent a bugle sable stringed or, on a chief azure three molets argent (Murray), 2nd and 3rd, Gules on a bend engrailed or a baton sable, within a bordure vair (Elliot), a chief of Augmentation above the quarterings, Argent a moor's head couped sable (Arms of Corsica)
Crest: From a duke's coronet or a pelican in her piety argent
Motto: De tout mon coeur
For Sir John Peter Boileau, 1st Bt., who m. 1825, Catherine Sarah, 3rd dau. of Gilbert, 1st Earl of Minto, and d. 9 Mar. 1869.   (B.P. 1939 ed.)

4. All black background
Argent a cross cotised of demi-fleurs-de-lys between four molets pierced sable (Atkyns)
Crest: Two greyhounds' heads addorsed, dexter argent, sinister sable, collared counterchanged   Motto: Vincent cum legebus arma
Unidentified

KIRBY CANE

1. All black background
Qly of six, 1st and 6th, Sable a wolf salient or in chief a fleur-de-lys argent between two bezants (Wilson), 2nd, Argent a bend within a bordure engrailed sable (Knyvett), 3rd, Argent a cross engrailed gules between four water bougets sable a label of three points azure, each point charged with a fleur-de-lys or (Bourchier), 4th, France quartering England, within a bordure argent (Holland, Earl of Kent), 5th, Qly or and azure (Fastolf)
Baron's coronet   Crest: A demi-wolf proper   Motto: Le bon temps viendra
Supporters: Dexter, A falcon rising wings elevated argent   Sinister, A greyhound proper
For the Rev. Henry Wilson, 10th Baron Berners, who d. 26 Feb. 1851. (B.P. 1949 ed.)

2. All black background
Vert a talbot's head erased argent between three garbs or (Crisp)
Crest: Issuant from a coronet of four horseshoes on a rim or on a mount vert a cock pheasant proper   Mantling: Vert and argent
Motto: Virtus e terra
For Major Raymond John Steffe Crisp, of Kirby Cane Hall, who d. 27 Nov. 1966.

KIRSTEAD
1. Dexter background black
Qly gules and sable a lion rampant argent between three annulets or
(Kerrison), impaling, Qly or and sable on a bend invected gules three
foxes' heads erased argent (Davis)
Crest: A dove argent winged or in its beak an olive branch proper
Mantling: Gules and argent   Motto: Quo mihi fortunam
For Sir Roger Kerrison, of Brooke, who m. 1765, Mary Ann, dau. of
Sylvester Davis, of Honnington, Suffolk, and d. 1808.   (B.L.G.
1937 ed.)

LANGLEY

1. All black background
Within the Order of the Bath, Qly, 1st and 4th, Argent a chevron sable
between three martlets gules (Proctor), 2nd and 3rd, Gules a fess
between six billets or a canton ermine (Beauchamp), over all the Badge
of Ulster
To dexter of main shield, Qly, 1st and 4th, Proctor, 2nd, Sable a tower
argent (Tower), 3rd, Beauchamp   A.Bl.   To sinister of main
shield, Qly, 1st and 4th, Proctor, 2nd and 3rd, Beauchamp   In
pretence: Or a water bouget sable, on a chief sable three bezants
(Johnson)   D. Bl.
Crest: A greyhound sejant proper collared or   Mantling: Gules and
argent
Motto: Toujours fidele   Supporters: Dexter, A wolf or   Sinister,
A greyhound proper collared or
For Sir William Beauchamp-Proctor, 1st Bt., who m. 1st, 1746, Jane,
dau. of Christopher Tower, of Huntsmore, Bucks, and 2nd, 1762,
Letitia, dau. and co-heir of Henry Johnson, of Great Berkhampstead,
Herts, and d. 13 Sept. 1773.   (B.P. 1875 ed.)

2. Dexter background black
Qly, 1st and 4th, Proctor, 2nd and 3rd, Beauchamp, over all the Badge
of Ulster, impaling, Qly, 1st and 4th, Chequy or and azure on a chief
gules two molets or (Palmer), 2nd and 3rd, Argent on a cross sable five
lions rampant or (Wakelin)
Crests: Dexter, On a mount vert a greyhound sejant proper collared or
Sinister, A tyger statant or vulned in the shoulder proper
Mantling and motto: As 1.
For Sir Thomas Beauchamp-Proctor, 2nd Bt., who m. 1778, Mary,
2nd dau. of Robert Palmer, of Sonning, Berks, and d. 29 Mar. 1827.
(B.P. 1939 ed.)

3. All black background
Arms: As 2, with Badge of Ulster
Crests, mantling and motto: As 2.

Presumably for Mary, widow of Sir Thomas Beauchamp-Proctor, 2nd
Bt.   She d. 25 Dec. 1847.   (B.P. 1939 ed.)
(The arms should be on a lozenge and without a crest)

4. All black background
Qly, 1st and 4th, Proctor, 2nd and 3rd, Beauchamp, over all the Badge
of Ulster   In pretence: Qly, 1st and 4th, Per pale azure and argent
two lions rampant addorsed counterchanged (Gregory), 2nd and 3rd,
Argent three lions passant guardant in pale gules (Brograve)
Crests and mantling: As 2.   Motto: Resurgam
Frame covered with black cloth   A particularly large hatchment
For Sir William Beauchamp-Proctor, 3rd Bt., who m. 1812, Anne, dau.
of Thomas Gregory, and niece and heir of Thomas Brograve, and d.
14 Mar. 1861.   (B.P. 1939 ed.)

LONG STRATTON

1. All black background
Argent two chevrons between three chaplets vert (Burroughes)   In
pretence: Or on a cross sable five crescents argent (Ellis)
Crest: A griffin's head erased argent charged with two chevrons vert
Mantling: Gules and argent   Motto: Resurgam
For the Rev. Randall Burroughes, who m. Elizabeth Maria, dau. and
heiress of William Ellis, of Kiddall Hall, Yorks, and d. 17 Sept. 1799.
(B.L.G. 1937 ed.)

2. Dexter background black
Qly, 1st and 4th, Burroughes, 2nd and 3rd, Ellis, impaling, Sable a
cross argent fretty sable between four lions' heads erased proper
langued gules (Marsh)
Crest, mantling and motto: As 1.
For the Rev. Ellis Burroughes, who m. 1795, Sarah Nasmyth, dau. of
Robert Marsh, of Norwich, and d. 24 Dec. 1831.   (B.L.G. 7th ed.)

MARLINGFORD

1. All black background
Ermine on a fess sable three lions rampant or (Rant)   In pretence: Or
on a bend between three martlets sable three hearts or (Life)
Crest: On a ducal coronet a lion sejant or   Mantling: Gules and
argent
Motto: In coelo quies   Skull below shield
For Humphrey Rant, of Dickleburgh, who m. Mary, dau. of Nathaniel
Life, of Marlingford, and d. 20 Jan, 1779.   (M.I. in church)
(This hatchment was recorded in 1953, but has since disappeared)

GREAT MASSINGHAM

1. Dexter background black
Gules a duck argent beaked and legged or (Langford)   In pretence:
Argent a lion rampant sable on a bend gules three escallops argent
(? Burnell)
Crest: A demi-duck wings elevated argent   Mantling: Gules and
argent
Motto: Mors janua vitae
For the Rev. H. S. E. C. Langford, Rector of Great Massingham,
who d. 17 Feb. 1789.   (M.I. in church)

MATLASK

1. Dexter background black
Azure a chevron or between three antelopes' heads erased argent
(Gunton)
In pretence: Per pale wavy argent and vert three greyhounds courant in
pale counterchanged a chief indented azure (Tomlinson/Thomlinson)
Crest: An antelope's head erased argent   Mantling: Gules and argent
Motto: Resurgam
Unidentified

2. All black background
On a curvilinear lozenge   Arms: As 1.
Unidentified

MULBARTON

1. Dexter background black
Qly argent and sable a cross between four escallops counterchanged
(Hooke), impaling, Azure a chevron engrailed ermine (Garrard)
Crest: An escallop sable between two wings argent   Mantling: Or
and argent
Motto: Curor ne cures
Unidentified

MUNDFORD

1. All black background
Qly, 1st and 4th, Argent a canton sable (Sutton), 2nd and 3rd, Argent a
cross flory sable (Lexington), over all the Badge of Ulster, impaling

Azure a cross engrailed or between four roses argent (Burton)
Crest: A wolf's head erased gules   Mantling: Gules and argent
Motto: Touts jours prest
For Sir Richard Sutton, 2nd Bt., who m. 1819, Mary Elizabeth, dau. of
Benjamin Burton, of Burton Hall, and d. 13 Nov. 1855.   (B.P.
1939 ed.)

2. Dexter and half sinister background black
Qly, 1st and 4th, Or on a chevron between three demi-lions rampant
gules a cross crosslet argent between two towers or (Stephens), 2nd and
3rd, Gules three stags' heads erased argent on a chief argent a cross
crosslet azure between two griffins' heads erased sable ermined argent
(Lyne)
Crests: Dexter, A raven's head ermine between two wings or, charged
on the neck with a tower or   Sinister, A griffin's head sable ermined
argent transfixed with a cross crosslet fitchy or   Mantling: Gules and
argent
Motto: Recte et suaviter
For Mr. S. Lyne-Stephens of Lynford Hall, who was lord of the
manor of East and West Hall in the parish of Mundford. He d.
(Farrer)

NARBOROUGH

1. Sinister background black
Qly, 1st and 4th, Or on a chevron vert between three French marigolds
slipped and leaved proper two lions rampant or (Tyssen), 2nd and 3rd,
Vert on a bend argent cotised or three tygers' heads erased affronté
gules (Bodicote), impaling, Sable a griffin segreant ermine winged or
(Baker)
Mantling: Gules and argent   Motto: In coelo quies
Cherub's head above shield
For Sophia, dau. of John Baker, of Deal, who m. Samuel Tyssen, of
Narborough Hall, and d. 19 July 1828.   (M.I. in church)

2. All black background
Arms: As 1. but chevron azure, tygers' heads not affronté and lions
combatant
Crest: A demi-lion or ducally crowned gules holding in its paws an
escutcheon azure charged with an estoile of six points or
Mantling: Gules and argent
Motto: Post mortem virtus virescit
Skull and crossbones and palm branches below shield
For Samuel Tyssen, who d. 1 Mar. 1845.   (M.I. in church)

NARFORD

1. All black background
Or a fess gules between three elephants' heads erased sable (Fountaine), impaling, Per pale indented argent and gules in the dexter chief a wolf's head erased sable (Penrice)
Crest: An elephant passant sable   Mantling: Gules and argent
Motto: Resurgam
For Andrew Fountaine, of Narford Hall, who m. 1805, Hannah, dau. of Thomas Penrice of Gt. Yarmouth, and d. 7 June 1835.   (B.L.G. 1937 ed.)

2. Sinister background black
Fountaine, impaling, Qly gules and azure over all a cross engrailed ermine (Berney)
Mantling: Gules and argent   Motto: Resurgam
Cherub's head above shield
For Caroline, dau. of Thomas Trench Berney, who m. 1848, Andrew Fountaine of Narford Hall, and d. 9 Aug. 1857.   (B.L.G. 1900 ed.)

3. All black background
Arms: As 3.
Crest: An elephant passant sable   Mantling: Gules and or
Motto: Resurgam
For Andrew Fountaine, who d. 11 Aug. 1874.   (B.L.G. 1900 ed.)
(As Narford is in a defence area the hatchments have been put temporarily into store)

NORWICH, St. John's R.C.

1. All black background
Qly, 1st, Argent three lozenge buckles gules (Jerningham), 2nd, qly, i. Gules on a bend between six cross crosslets fitchy argent an escutcheon or charged with a demi-lion rampant pierced through the mouth by an arrow within a double tressure flory-counterflory gules (Howard), ii. Gules three lions passant guardant in pale or in chief a label of three points argent (Brotherton), iii. Chequy or and azure (Warren), iv. Gules a lion rampant argent (Mowbray), 3rd, Qly France and England a bordure argent (Woodstock), 4th, Or a chevron gules (Stafford), over all a molet for difference, impaling, Argent fretty and a canton sable (Middleton)
Crest: From a ducal coronet a demi-falcon or   Mantling: Gules and argent
Motto: Virtus basis vitae
For Edward Jerningham, of Painswick, who m. 1804, Emily, dau. of Nathaniel Middleton, and d. 29 May 1822.   (B.P. 1939 ed.)
(Possibly also used for his widow, who d. 24 June 1822)

2. Dexter background black
Dexter, as 1., with Badge of Ulster, impaling, Argent a lion passant between three crescents gules (Dillon)
Crest: From a ducal coronet or a demi-falcon proper
Mantling: Gules and argent   Motto: Virtus basis vitae
Palm branches flanking shield
For Sir William Jerningham, 6th Bt., who. m. 1767, Frances, eldest dau. of Henry, 11th Viscount Dillon, and d. 14 Aug. 1809.   (B.P. 1939 ed).

3. All black background
On a lozenge   Arms: As 5.
No crest, mantling or motto
For Frances, widow of Sir William Jerningham, 6th Bt.   She d. 1 Mar. 1825.   (B.P. 1939 ed.)

4. Sinister background black
Dexter, as 1., with Badge of Ulster   In pretence: Argent a chevron gules between three pheons sable (Sulyard)
Baroness's coronet   Mantling: Gules and ermine   Motto: Abstulit qui dedit
Supporters: Dexter, A lion argent charged on the shoulder with a crescent sable   Sinister, A swan argent beaked proper feet sable ducally gorged per pale gules and sable
For Frances Henrietta, dau. and co-heir of Edward Sulyard, of Haughley Park, who m. as his 1st wife, George William, 8th Baron Stafford, and d. 14 Nov. 1832.   (B.P. 1939 ed.)

5. Dexter background black
Dexter, as 1., with Badge of Ulster, impaling, Argent a sword erect hilted or between two lions combatant gules (Caton)
Baron's coronet   Crests (above coronet): Dexter, From a ducal coronet a demi-falcon or   Sinister, From a ducal coronet per pale gules and sable a swan argent
Motto and supporters: As 2.
For George William, 8th Baron Stafford, who m. 2nd, 1836, Elizabeth, dau. of Richard Caton, of Maryland, and d. 4 Oct. 1851.   (B.P. 1939 ed.)

6. Sinister background black
Dexter, as 1., with Badge of Ulster, impaling, Howard qly as dexter
Baroness's coronet over the Stafford knot or   Motto and supporters: As 4, but lion has no crescent, and swan has beak and feet gules
For Julia Barbara, dau. of John Edward Charles Howard, 1st wife of Henry Valentine, 9th Baron Stafford.   She d. 19 Nov. 1856.   (B.P. 1939 ed.)

NORWICH, Old Meeting House

1. All black background

Argent a garb between three pairs of logs in saltire proper, in chief a shed gules (Stackhouse)

Crest: Two logs in saltire proper   Mantling: Gules and argent

Inscribed (around frame): The Rev. John Stackhouse, d. Sept. 14, 1707, aged 69 years

(This hatchment, last recorded in 1953, is now missing)

NORWICH, St. Peter Mancroft

1. All black background

On a lozenge   Or a bend gules over all a fess azure (Elwes)

Unidentified

OXBURGH Hall

1. Dexter background black

Qly, 1st and 4th, Ermine an eagle displayed gules (Bedingfeld), 2nd and 3rd, Lozengy argent and gules (Tuddenham), over all the Badge of Ulster, impaling, Qly, 1st, Or a chevron gules (Stafford), 2nd, Qly France and England a bordure argent (Plantagenet), 3rd, Gules on a bend between six cross crosslets fitchy argent an escutcheon or charged with a demi-lion rampant pierced through the mouth by an arrow within a double tressure flory-counter-flory gules (Howard), 4th, Argent three lozenge buckles clasps fesswise gules (Jerningham)

Crest: An eagle displayed or   Mantling: Gules and argent

Motto: Despicio terrena solem contemplor

For Sir Richard Bedingfeld, 5th Bt., who m. 1795, Charlotte Georgiana, dau. of Sir William Jerningham, 6th Bt. of Costessey, and d. 22 Nov. 1829.   (B.P. 1939 ed.)

2. All black background

On a lozenge surmounted by a cherub's head

Qly, 1st and 4th, Bedingfeld, 2nd and 3rd, Tuddenham, over all the Badge of Ulster, impaling, Qly, 1st, Jerningham, 2nd, Howard, 3rd, Plantagenet, 4th, Stafford

For Charlotte Georgiana, widow of Sir Richard Bedingfeld, 5th Bt. She d. 29 July 1854.   (B.P. 1939 ed.)

3. Dexter background black

Qly, 1st, Bedingfeld, 2nd, Argent three pallets azure, on a bend gules three eagles displayed or (Grandison), 3rd, Tuddenham, 4th, Argent a fess sable between three crescents gules (Pateshall), over all the Badge

of Ulster   In pretence: Argent six fleurs-de-lys, three, two, one
azure a chief indented or (Paston)
Crests: Dexter, as 1.   Sinister, A plume of peacocks' feathers proper
Motto: As 1.   Supporters: Dexter, A bear proper, collared, muzzled
and chained or   Sinister, An ostrich proper in its beak a horseshoe or
Below the shield the Order of St. John of Jerusalem
For Sir Henry Richard Paston-Bedingfeld, 6th Bt., who m. 1826, Margaret Anne, only child and heir of Edward Paston, and d. 4 Feb.
1862.   (B.P. 1939 ed.)

LITTLE PLUMSTEAD

1. **All black background**
Per pale indented argent and gules in dexter chief a wolf's head couped
sable (Penrice)
Crest: A pair of wings argent the sinister charged with two molets
gules
Mantling: Gules and argent   Motto: Resurgam
Probably for Thomas Penrice, of Great Yarmouth, who d. 11 Nov.
1816.   (Farrer)

2. **All black background**
Argent a chevron between three molets pierced azure (Columbine),
impaling, Per fess argent and azure a molet of eight points pierced
counterchanged (Skottowe)
Crest: A dove proper   Mantling: Gules and argent
Motto: In Christo stat unica salus
For the Rev. Paul Colombine, Rector of Little Plumstead, who m. 2nd,
Katharine Skottowe, and d. 18 Nov. 1821.   (Farrer; E. R. Granger)

3. **Sinister background black**
Qly, 1st and 4th, Gules a cross engrailed argent (Leigh), 2nd, Or a lion
rampant gules (   ), 3rd, Azure two bars argent a bend counter-
compony or and gules (Leigh), impaling two coats per pale, Or five
chevrons azure (Evering), and, Qly, 1st, Argent three Moors' heads
couped proper wreathed at the temples argent and azure (? Canning),
2nd, Gules three cronels in fess or (   ), 3rd, Sable a goat rampant
or (   ), 4th, Azure three bendlets or a bordure engrailed gules
(   )
Crest: A unicorn's head erased sable, armed and maned or, collared
gules bezanty   Motto: Tout vient de Dieu
Probably for the second wife of the Rev. William Leigh, of Rushall,
Staffs, Rector of Little Plumstead.   He d. 11 Aug. 1808.   (Farrer)

EAST RAYNHAM

1; Dexter background black
Qly of sixteen, 1st, Azure a chevron ermine between three escallops
argent (Townshend), 2nd, Qly gules and argent in the first quarter a
molet argent, a crescent for difference (Vere), 3rd, Sable a lion
passant or between three esquires' helmets argent (Compton), 4th,
Paly of six or and azure a canton ermine (Shirley), 5th, Argent a fess
and in chief three annulets gules (Devereux), 6th, Vairy or and gules
(Ferrers), 7th, Azure three garbs or (Chester), 8th, Or an eagle displayed sable (   ), 9th, Gules seven lozenges three, three, and one or
(Ferrers), 10th, Gules a cinquefoil ermine (Beaumont), 11th, Gules a
pale or (   ), 12th, Or a lion rampant within a tressure flory-counter-
flory gules (   ), 13th, Argent a cross engrailed between four water
bougets sable (Bourchier), 14th, Argent a lion rampant sable (Louvaine),
15th, France quartering England within a bordure argent (Plantagenet),
16th, Azure a bend argent cotised or between six lions rampant or
(Bohun), impaling, Or a fess chequy argent and azure within a double
tressure flory-counter-flory gules (Stuart)
Marquess's coronet   Crest: A stag proper   Motto: Haec generi
incrementa fides   Supporters: Dexter, A stag sable attired or
Sinister, A greyhound argent
For John, 4th Marquess Townshend, who m. 1825, Elizabeth Jane, dau,
of Rear-Admiral Lord George Stuart, and d. 10 Sept. 1863.
(B.P. 1939 ed.)
(There is another hatchment for the 4th Marquess at Tamworth Castle,
Staffs)

RINGLAND

1. All black background
Argent on a cross sable five fleurs-de-lys argent (Le Neve), impaling, Or
on a bend sable three leopards' faces argent (Mingay)
Crest: From a ducal coronet or a lily argent stalked and leaved vert
Mantling: Gules and argent
Skull and crossbones on frame
For Peter Le Neve, who m. Anna Eliza, dau. of William Mingay, of
Norwich, and d. 18 Oct. 1766, aged 45.   She d. 15 Sept. 1891, aged
44.   (Farrer)
(In view of the background this hatchment may have also been used for
his widow)

2. Dexter background black
Le Neve, impaling, Argent a fess wavy between three molets sable
(Blackborne)
Crest and mantling: As 1.
Skulls and crossbones on frame

For Francis Le Neve, who m. Anne, dau. of Henry Blackborne, of
Wymondham, and d. 5 Dec. 1708, aged 67.   She d. 6 Nov. 1721,
aged 77.   (Farrer)

NORTH RUNCTON

1. **Sinister background black**
Argent a cross engrailed gules in the first quarter a bell sable (Gurney),
impaling, Argent three escutcheons gules (Hay)
Cherub's head above shield, and ears of corn below
For Harriet Jemima, dau. of William, 17th Earl of Erroll, who m.
Daniel Gurney, and d. 8 Feb. 1837.   (B.L.G. 1937 ed.)

RYSTON

1. **All black background**
On a lozenge   Argent on a chevron between three roundels sable, the
two in chief each charged with a martlet argent and the one in base
with a trefoil slipped argent, three mascles argent (Pratt), impaling,
Azure a cinquefoil pierced ermine a bordure engrailed or (Astley)
Mantling: Gules and argent   Motto: Resurgam
For Blanche, dau. of Sir Jacob Astley, 3rd Bt., of Melton Constable,
who m. Edward Pratt of Ryston, and d. 8 May 1805.   (B.L.G.
1937 ed.)

2. **Sinister background black**
Pratt   In pretence: Argent a double-headed eagle displayed sable
(Browne)
Motto: In coelo quies   Two cherubs' heads above shield
For Pleasance, dau. and co-heir of Samuel Browne, of Kings Lynn, who
m. Edward Roger Pratt, of Ryston, and d. 3 Oct. 1807.   (B.L.G.
1937; Farrer)

3. **All black background**
Qly, 1st and 4th, Pratt, 2nd and 3rd, Sable on a chevron argent between
three birds' heads erased ermine three annulets sable (Gylour)   In
pretence: Browne
Crest: A wolf's head per pale argent and sable gorged with a collar
charged with three roundels counterchanged, between an oak sprig and
a pine sprig proper   Mantling: Gules and argent   Motto: Rident
florentia prata
For Edward Roger Pratt, who d. 5 Mar. 1838.   (B.L.G. 1937 ed.;
Farrer)

SALHOUSE

1. Dexter background black
Argent on a bend engrailed sable between two acorns slipped vert
three fleurs-de-lys or (Ward), impaling, Azure two bars wavy argent
(Brooksbank)
Crest: A dexter arm erect couped at the elbow habited qly or and vert
cuffed argent the hand proper holding a pheon point downwards argent
Mantling: Gules and or   Motto: Loyal till death   Skull below
For Richard Ward, of Walcot and Salhouse, who m. Amelia, dau. of
Stamp Brooksbank, M.P. and d. 1799.   (B.L.G. 1937 ed.)

2. Sinister background black
Ward, impaling, Sable three swords in pale argent pommelled and hilted
or the centre one pommel in base (Rawle)
Cherub's head above shield
For Lydia, dau. of Richard Rawle, of Liskeard, Cornwall, who m. as his
first wife, Robert Ward, of Salhouse Hall, and d. 7 Jan. 1839.
(B.L.G. 1937 ed.)

3 Dexter and part sinister background black
Ward, impaling, two coats per pale, 1st, Rawle, 2nd, Per chief sable and
or a bend engrailed gules charged with three bezants (Hallett)
Crest and mantling: As 1.   Motto: Usque ad mortem fidus
For Robert Ward, of Salhouse Hall, who m. 1st, Lydia, dau. of Richard
Rawle, of Liskeard, Cornwall, and 2nd, – Hallett, and d. 14 Feb. 1843.
(B.L.G. 1937 ed.)

SALL

1. All black background
Ermine a fess engrailed between three lions rampant or (Hase)   In
pretence: Ermine three chevronels azure (Repps)
Crest: A falcon rising ermine   Mantling: Gules and argent
Motto: Resurgam
For Edward Hase, of Sall, who m. 1754, Virtue, dau. of John Repps of
Matishall, and d. 11 May 1804.   (Foster's 'Peerage', 1880;   Farrer)

2. Sinister background
Qly, 1st and 4th, Sable ermined argent a trefoil slipped or between
three round buckles argent (Jodrell), 2nd and 3rd, Argent on a chevron
gules three sheldrakes argent on a canton gules a rose argent (Sheldon),
impaling, Hase
Motto: Sunt lachrymae rerum   Cherubs' heads above shield
For Virtue, dau. of Edward Hase of Sall, who m. Richard Paul Jodrell, of
Saxlingham, and d. 23 March, 1806. (Foster's 'Peerage', 1880;   Farrer)

3. All black background
Qly, 1st, Jodrell, with trefoil argent, 2nd, Or on a fess dancetty between three billets azure each charged with a lion rampant or three bezants (Rolle), 3rd, Sheldon, 4th, qly i. and iv., qly 1. and 4., Per bend dancetty argent and sable, 2. and 3., Azure a fleur-de-lys or (Warner), ii. and iii., Vert a cross engrailed argent (Whetenhall)   In pretence: Qly, 1st, Hase, 2nd, Repps, 3rd, Or a bend between three trefoils slipped azure (? Smythe), 4th, Azure two weaving combs in fess between two halves of a broken tilting spear or (Lombe)
Crest: A demi-cockatrice wings erect or issuing from a chaplet of roses gules   Mantling: Gules and argent   Motto: Mentem mortalia tangunt
For Richard Paul Jodrell, who d. 26 Jan. 1831.   (Foster's 'Peerage', 1880;   Farrer)

SANDRINGHAM

1. All black background
Qly, 1st and 4th, England, 2nd, Scotland, 3rd, Ireland
The shield surrounded with the Garter and surmounted by an imperial crown
On a wood panel, c. 2ft. 6in. x 2ft. 6in.   Used on the royal train
For H.M. King George V, d. 20 Jan. 1936

2. Identical to 1.   Also used on the royal train
For H.M. King George VI, d. 6 Feb. 1952

SCOTTOW

1. All black background
Argent a chevron between three garbs sable (Blake), impaling, Ermine on a fess gules three bezants (Clarke)
Crest: On a chapeau gules and ermine a swallow proper
Mantling: Gules and argent   Skull below shield
For Thomas Blake, of Scottow, who m. 1754, Judith, dau. of William Clarke, of Loddon, and d. 26 June 1806.   (B.L.G. 7th ed.)

2. All black background
Or ermined sable a cross crosslet sable ermined argent (Durrant)
Crest: A boar passant per fess argent and gules
Mantling: Gules and argent   No motto
Unidentified

3. All black background
Arms, crest and mantling: As 2.
Motto: Resurgam
Unidentified

4. All black background
Durrant   In pretence.   Durrant
On a shield surmounted by a skull
For Davy Durrant, who m. Margaret, dau. of Thomas Durrant, and d.
22 Sept. 1759.   (Farrer)

5. Dexter background black
Durrant, with Badge of Ulster in dexter chief, impaling, Or an eagle
displayed gules charged with an estoile of six points or (Custance)
Crest: As 2.   Motto: Labes perjor morte
For Sir Thomas Durrant, 1st Bt., who m. Susanna, dau. of Hambleton
Custance, of Weston, and d. 30 Aug. 1790.   (Farrer)

6. All black background
On a lozenge surmounted by a cherub's head
Arms: As 5., with Badge of Ulster in sinister chief
For Susanna, widow of Sir Thomas Durrant, 1st Bt.   She d. 9 Dec.
1833.   (Farrer)

7. Dexter background black
Durrant, with Badge of Ulster in centre chief, impaling, Argent a goat
rampant proper (? Steenbergen)
Crest and mantling: As 2.   Motto: As 5.
For Sir Thomas Durrant, 2nd Bt., who m. 1799, Sarah Crooke, dau. of
Henry Steenbergen, of the Island of St. Christopher, and d. 22 May
1829.   (B.P. 1939 ed.)

8. All black background
On a lozenge   Arms: As 7., with Badge of Ulster in chief
Mantling: Gules and argent   Motto: As 5.
For Sarah, widow of Sir Thomas Durrant, 2nd Bt.   She d. July 1845.
(B.P. 1939 ed.)

9, Dexter background black
Durrant, with Badge of Ulster in chief (over impalement line), impaling,
Ermine on a cross engrailed between four eagles displayed gules five
cinquefoils or (Stracey)
Crest and mantling: As 2.   Motto: Resurgam
For Sir Henry Thomas Estridge Durrant, 3rd Bt., who m. 2nd, 1833,
Diana Julia, dau. of Sir Josias Henry Stracey, 4th Bt., and d. 16 May
1861.   (B.P. 1939 ed.)

10. All brown background
Qly, 1st and 4th, Argent a chevron sable ermined or, on a canton gules
an eagle's head erased or (Shaw), 2nd and 3rd, Durrant
Crest: A talbot statant proper   Motto: Mens immota manet
For Colonel Geoffrey Reginald Devereux Shaw, who d. 8 Sept. 1960.
(B.L.G. 1972 ed.)

SCOULTON

1. Identical to Woodrising No. 2 (q.v.)

SIDESTRAND

1. Dexter background black
Two shields   Dexter, within the Order of the Star of India, Sable a
double-headed eagle within a bordure indented argent, in centre chief
the Badge of Ulster (Hoare)   Sinister, within the Order of the
British Empire, Argent two lions passant in pale tails forked gules
armed and langued azure (Lygon)
Viscount's coronet (below crest)   Crest: A stag's head erased argent
charged with a cross couped sable   Mantling: Sable and argent
Motto: Hora venit   Supporters: Two stags or each charged on the
shoulder with a cross couped sable.   Pendent below dexter shield
badge of the Order of the Star of India, also Star of Order of British
Empire, and Star of Order of the Bath (should be Order of St. Michael
and St. George, from which ribbon it hangs)   Pendent below sinister
shield Star of the Order of the British Empire
For Samuel, 1st Viscount Templewood, who m. 1909, Lady Maud
Lygon, D.B.E., dau. of 6th Earl Beauchamp, and d. 7 May 1959.
(B.P. 1970 ed.)

SLOLEY Hall

1. All black background
On an oval surmounted by a cherub's head   Two coats per fess
In chief, Vert three greyhounds courant argent, on a chief argent three
buglehorns sable stringed gules (Hunter), and in base, Sable a chevron
invected vair between three lions rampant or each holding an escutcheon argent charged with an eagle's head erased azure, in dexter chief
the Badge of Ulster (Neville), impaling, Qly, 1st, Sable a shin bone in
pale surmounted by another in fess argent between two crosses formy
in bend or (Baines), 2nd, Argent a bend sable on a chief sable three
woolsacks argent (Johnson), 3rd, Argent a fess sable between in chief a
demi-lion rampant issuant and in base three molets of six points azure

(Oeils), 4th, Argent on a fess gules a cross formy between two cross
crosslets fitchy or (Cuthbert)
For Violet Sophia Mary, dau. of Lt.-Col. Cuthbert Johnson Baines, who
m. 1st, Captain R. J. Hunter, and 2nd, Sir Reginald James Neville,
1st Bt., and d. Aug. 1972.   (B.P. 1949 ed.)

SNETTISHAM

1. Dexter background black
Sable a unicorn passant or, on a chief or three billets sable (Styleman),
impaling, Gules two lions passant argent (L'Estrange)
Crest: A camel's head erased proper bezanty, muzzled, collared and
corded or   Mantling: Gules and argent   Motto: In coelo quies
For Nicholas Styleman, who m. Armine, dau. and co-heir of Sir
Nicholas L'Estrange, and d. 6 Jan. 1746.   (Farrer)

2. All black background
On a lozenge   Arms: As 1., but unicorn statant
Motto: In coelo quies
For Armine, widow of Nicholas Styleman.   She d. 29 May 1768.
(Farrer)

3. Dexter background black
Styleman, as 2., impaling, Azure a lion rampant argent ducally crowned
or within a bordure argent charged with eight roundels sable (Henley)
Crest and mantling: As 1.   Motto: Spes in Deo
For Nicholas Styleman, who m. Catherine, dau. of Henry Holt Henley,
of Leigh, Somerset, and d. 9 Jan. 1788.   (Farrer; B.L.G. 5th ed.)

4. All black background
Styleman, as 2., impaling, Sable a chevron ermine between three
leopards' faces or (Blakeway)
Crest and mantling: As 1.   Motto: Mors janua vitae
For the Rev. Armine Styleman, who m. Ann, dau. of James Blakeway,
and d. 3 Apr. 1803.   (B.L.G. 5th ed.)

5. Sinister background black
Styleman, as 2.   In pretence: Argent on a chevron sable three
trefoils slipped argent (Gregg)
Mantling: Gules and argent   Motto: In coelo quies
Cherub's head above shield
For Mary, dau. of Robert Gregg, who m. as his 1st wife, Henry Style-
man, and d. 7 Dec. 1807.   (B.L.G. 5th ed.; N. P. Wood)

6. Dexter and top sinister background black
Qly, 1st and 4th, Styleman, as 2., 2nd and 3rd, Gules two lions passant
argent over all a bend or (L'Estrange), impaling, two coats per fess:

1. Gregg   2. Gules a fess between three lions' heads erased or (Preedy)
Crest, mantling and motto: As 1.
For Henry Styleman, who m. 1st, 1780, Mary, dau. of Robert Gregg,
and 2nd, 1809, Emilia, dau. of Benjamin Preedy, of St. Albans, and d.
25 Mar. 1819.   (B.L.G. 1937 ed.)

STOW BARDOLPH

1. Dexter background black
Gules two bars and a chief indented or, the Badge of Ulster (Hare),
impaling, Argent a chevron between three crosses formy gules (Newby)
Crest: A demi-lion rampant argent ducally gorged or
For Sir Thomas Hare, 4th Bt., who m. Rosamond, dau. of Charles
Newby of Hooton, Yorks, and d. 21 Feb. 1760.   (B.P. 1939 ed.)

2. Sinister background black
Hare, impaling, Qly, 1st and 4th, Gules on two bars or three mascles
two and one azure, on a canton argent an anchor with cable erect sable
(Geary), 2nd and 3rd, Argent two chevronels between three fleurs-de-
lys gules a bordure sable (Geary)
Motto: In coelo quies
For Mary, dau. of Admiral Sir Francis Geary, Bt., who m. as his 1st
wife, 1779, Sir Thomas Hare, 1st Bt.   She d. 23 Nov.1801.
(Farrer; B.P. 1939 ed.)

3. Sinister background black
Hare, with Badge of Ulster, impaling, Qly, 1st and 4th, Gules an eagle
displayed or ducally crowned argent on a canton argent an anchor
erect sable (Graves), 2nd and 3rd, Gules from a cave a wolf emerging
reguardant proper (Williams)
Motto: In coelo quies   Shield surmounted by two cherubs' heads
For Anne Elizabeth, dau. of Thomas, 1st Lord Graves, who m. as his
2nd wife, Sir Thomas Hare, 1st Bt.   She d. 11 Sept. 1823.
(Sources, as 2.)

4. All black background
Arms: as 3.
Crest: As 1.   Mantling: Gules and argent   Motto: In coelo quies
For Sir Thomas Hare, 1st Bt., who d. 12 Feb. 1834.   (Sources, as 2.)

SWANNINGTON

1. All black background
On a lozenge surmounted by a cherub's head

Qly, 1st and 4th, Argent a lion passant guardant gules imperially crowned and gorged or (Ogilvie), 2nd and 3rd, Argent a cross engrailed sable (Sinclair), impaling, Per pale argent and gules a lion rampant sable (Bladwell)
For Maria Barbara Bladwell, who m. General George Ogilvie, and d. (Farrer)

2. All black background
Qly, 1st and 6th, Bladwell, 2nd, Gules a fess wavy ermine (   ), 3rd, Argent a fess between two chevrons gules (Peche), 4th, Gules a chevron flory argent (   ), 5th, Argent on a chevron between three crows sable three cinquefoils argent (Caldebeck)
Crest: A demi-lion rampant sable   Mantling: Gules and argent
Palm branches flanking base of shield
Unidentified

3. All black background
Arms: As 2., but crescent for difference in 1st quarter
Crest and mantling: As 2.   Motto: In coelo quies
Unidentified

TACOLNESTON

1. Sinister background black
Sable two bars and in chief three wolves' heads erased argent langued gules (Knipe)   In pretence: Or on a cross gules five molets argent (Burroughes)
Crest: A wolf's head erased argent langued gules transfixed by an arrow or
For Mary, dau. and co-heiress of Henry Burroughes, who m. Edmund Knipe, and d.   He d. 2 Mar. 1703, aged 82.   (Farrer)

2. All black background
Azure a castle triple-towered and in base a crescent or (Boileau)   In pretence: Azure on a bend between six lozenges or each charged with an escallop azure five escallops azure (Pollen)
Crest: A pelican in her piety proper, charged on the breast with a saltire couped gules, the nest resting on a foreign coronet or
Mantling: Gules and argent   Motto: De tout mon coeur
For John Peter Boileau, who m. 1790, Henrietta, dau. and co-heir of the Rev. George Pollen, of Little Bookham, and d. 10 Mar. 1837. (B.P. 1939 ed.)

TERRINGTON ST. CLEMENTS

1. Dexter background black

Argent on a chevron between in chief two roundels sable each charged
with a martlet argent and in base an oak wreath proper three escallops
or, a bordure engrailed vert, in chief the Badge of Ulster (Hamond)
In pretence: Or three roses within a bordure gules on a chief sable three
escallops or (Graeme)
Crest: From a naval coronet or, sails argent, an eagle's head sable
beaked or   Mantling: Gules and argent   Motto: Paratus et fidelis
For Sir Andrew Snape Hamond, 1st Bt., who m. 1779, Anne, dau, and
heir of Henry Graeme, of Hanwell, and d. 12 Sept. 1828.   (B.P.
1890 ed.; Farrer)

2. All black background

On a lozenge   Arms: As 1., but with arms in pretence on a lozenge
For Anne, widow of Sir Andrew Snape Hamond, 1st Bt.   She d. 7
Sept. 1838.   (B.P. 1890 ed.; Farrer)

TIBENHAM

1. Sinister background black

Qly, 1st and 4th, Argent a lion rampant the tail over the head sable
(Buxton), 2nd and 3rd, Or two stags lodged gules attired sable
(Buxton), impaling, Or on a canton sable a tiger's head erased or
(Jacob)
Crest: A buck's head erased proper   Motto: Servare modum
Cherub's head below shield
For Elizabeth, dau. and co-heiress of John Jacob, of the Rocks, Gloucs,
who m. John Buxton of Shadwell Lodge, and d. 10 Nov. 1765.
(Farrer)

TITTLESHALL

1. Dexter background black

Per pale gules and azure three eagles displayed argent (Coke), impaling,
Gules three escallops argent (Keppel)
Earl's coronet   Crest: On a chapeau azure and ermine an ostrich
argent in its beak a horse shoe or   Mantling: Gules and argent
Motto: Resurgam   Supporters: Two ostriches proper ducally gorged
and lined or
For Thomas William, 1st Earl of Leicester, who m. 2nd, Anne Amelia,
dau. of William, 4th Earl of Albermarle, and d. 30 June 1842.
(B.P. 1939 ed.)
(There is an identical hatchment in the parish church at Longford,

Derbyshire; the other five hatchments recorded by Farrer are probably
still in the mausoleum on the north side of the chancel which has been
bricked up for many years.)

TOFTREES

1. Dexter background black
Lozengy or and azure a canton ermine (Buck), impaling, Qly, 1st and
4th, Argent two lions gambs in chevron couped gules between three
hawks' lures proper (? Chester), 2nd and 3rd, Per fess gules and argent
six martlets counterchanged (? Fenwick)
Crest: A Saracen's head and shoulders in profile proper, vested or and
azure, cap or, wreathed at the temples or and azure, collared with two
bars gemel or   Mantling: Azure and or   Below the shield pendent
the cross of a Knight of St. John of Jerusalem
For the Rev. John Parmenter Buck, Vicar of Toftrees, who m. Jane,
and d. 19 Jan. 1861.   (Farrer; M.I. in churchyard)

TOPCROFT

1. Dexter background black
Sable on a chevron engrailed between six crosses formy fitchy or three
fleurs-de-lys azure (Smyth), impaling, Argent a galley proper (   )
Crest: A heron's head erased argent in its beak a fish proper
Mantling: Gules and argent
For John Smyth, of Cringleford Hall, who m. Eliza, and d. 14 June
1808.   (Farrer)

2. All black background
On a lozenge surmounted by a cherub's head
Arms: As 1.
Mantling: Gules and or   Skull below
For Eliza, widow of John Smyth.   She d. 3 Feb. 1842.   (Farrer)

WALPOLE ST. PETER

1. All black background
Sable a fess cotised between three conies argent (Cony), impaling,
Argent three pallets azure over all a chevron gules charged with a
crescent or for difference (Barkham)
Crest: A demi-coney holding in the dexter paw a pansy or leaved vert
Motto: Pars pari
For Robert Cony, who m. Alice, dau of Sir Robert Barkham, of
Wainfleet, Lincs, and d. 5 Apr. 1707.   (Farrer)

2. All black background
Cony, impaling, Sable a chevron ermine between three millrinds or, on
a chief argent a lion passant gules (Turner)
Crest: As 1.   Mantling: Gules and argent   Motto: As 1.
For Edwin Cony, who m. Elizabeth, dau. of Charles Turner, of Kings
Lynn, and d. 23 Sept. 1755.   (Farrer)

LITTLE WALSINGHAM

The following seven hatchments, last recorded in 1952, were destroyed
in the fire on the night of 14th July 1961.

1. All black background (should be S.Bl.)
Qly, 1st and 4th, Gules a fess compony or and azure between eight
billets or (Lee), 2nd, Qly, i. and iv. Per pale indented argent and azure,
ii. and iii. Azure a fleur-de-lys or (Warner), 3rd, Vert a cross engrailed
argent (Whetenhall), impaling, Argent a fess between three wolves'
heads couped sable (Howe)
Mantling: Gules and argent
For Dorothy, dau. of Sir George Grubham Howe, Bt., of Berwick St.
Leonard, Wiltshire, who m. Henry Lee, of Donjon, near Canterbury,
and d. 27 July, 1727.   (B.L.G. 1937 ed.:   Farrer)

2. All black background
Arms: As 1.
Crest: A squirrel sejant between two branches proper
Mantling: Gules and argent
For Henry Lee, who d. 6 Sept. 1734, aged 76.   (Sources, as 1.)

3. Dexter background black
Qly, 1st, Lee, 2nd, Warner, 3rd, Whetenhall, 4th, Howe, impaling,
Ermine a millrind sable (Milles)
Motto: Non nobis tantum nati
For Henry Lee-Warner, of Walsingham Abbey, who m. Mary, dau. of
Samuel Milles, of Nackington, Kent, and d. 13 Dec. 1760.   (Sources,
as 1.)

4. All black background
On a lozenge   Arms: As 3.
Motto: As 3.
For Mary, widow of Henry Lee-Warner.   She d.   (Sources, as 1.)

5. All black background
Qly of six, 1st and 6th, Lee, 2nd Warner, 3rd, Whetenhall, 4th, Howe,
5th, Vert three leaves or (Woodward)   In pretence: Or ermined
sable three scimitars argent hilted or (Howarth)

Crest and mantling: As 2.   Motto: Resurgam
For Daniel Henry Lee-Warner, who m. 1774, Margaret, dau. and heir of
Nathaniel Haworth, and d. 1835.   (Sources, as 1.)

6. Dexter background black
Qly of six, 1st, Lee, 2nd, Warner, 3rd, Whetenhall, 4th, Howe, 5th,
Woodward, 6th, Howarth   In pretence: Argent on a cross sable a
leopard's face or (Brydges)
Crest: As 2.   Motto: As 3.
For the Rev. Daniel Henry Lee-Warner, who m. 1808, Ann, eldest dau.
and co-heir of Francis William Thomas Brydges, of Tyberton Court,
Hereford, and d. 1858.   (Sources, as 1.)
(There is an identical hatchment, except for the motto, in the parish
church at Tyberton, Herefordshire)

7. All black background
Qly, 1st, Lee, 2nd, Warner, 3rd, Whetenhall, 4th, Howe
Crest: As 2.   Motto: As 3.
Probably for Henry Lee-Warner, who d. unm. 12 July 1804, aged 81.
(Sources, as 1.)

WARHAM ST. MARY

1. Sinister background black (recorded in 1952 as all black)
Sable a chevron ermine between three millrinds or, on a chief argent a
lion passant gules, the Badge of Ulster (Turner), impaling, Gules a bend
vair between two fleurs-de-lys argent (Blois)
Crest: A lion passant gules in the dexter paw a laurel branch proper
Mantling: Gules and argent
Frame decorated with skulls and crossbones
Probably for both Sir Charles Turner, 1st Bt., and his second wife,
Mary, dau. of Sir William Blois, of Cockfield Hall.   She d. 30 Aug.
1738.   He d. 24 Nov. 1738.   (B.E.B.: mon. in church)

2. Dexter background black
Turner, with Badge of Ulster, impaling, Azure a cross potent or (Allen)
Crest: As 1.   Mantling: Gules and argent   Motto: Non omnis
morior
For Sir John Turner, 2nd Bt., who m. Anne, dau. of Thomas Allen, of
London, and d. 6 Jan. 1739.   (B.E.B.: Farrer)

3. Sinister background black
Turner (lion holds a laurel branch proper), with Badge of Ulster.   In
pretence: Per pale sable and gules a lion passant guardant argent (Neale)
Crest and mantling: As 1.   Frame decorated with skulls and

crossbones
For Frances, dau. and co-heir of John Neale, of Allesley, Warwickshire,
who m. Sir John Turner, 3rd, Bt., and d. Mar. 1748.   (B.E.B.;
Farrer)

4. All black background
Arms: As 3.
Crest and mantling: As 1.   Motto: Resurgam
Palm branches flanking shield
For Sir John Turner, 3rd Bt., who d. June 1780.   (B.E:B.;   Farrer)

WATLINGTON

1. All black background
On a lozenge   Qly, 1st and 4th, Gules a lion rampant between two
bendlets or (Plestow), 2nd and 3rd, Qly or and vert (Berners)   In
pretence: Sable on a chevron between three hinds trippant argent three
annulets sable (Collett)
Unidentified

2. Dexter background black
Qly, 1st and 4th, Plestow, 2nd, Berners, 3rd, Collett, impaling, Azure
six annulets, three two, and one or (Musgrave)
Crest: From a ducal coronet or a lion's head argent
Mantling: Gules and argent   Motto: Spes in Deo
Cherub's head below shield
For Charles Berners Plestow, who d. 29 May 184(3), aged 52.
(Farrer)

WATTON

1. All black background
Gules a fess wavy between three fleurs-de-lys or, a crescent for dif-
ference   (Hicks)
Crest: A stag's head or collared gules   Mantling: Gules and argent
Skull below shield   A small hatchment, c. 2ft. 6in. x 2ft. 6in.
For the Rev. William Hicks, Vicar of Watton, who d. 26 Oct. 1784.
(Farrer)

WESTACRE

1. Dexter backgroundd black
Azure three doves proper between two chevronels or (Hamond), impaling,
Qly sable and or in the first quarter a cinquefoil argent (Packe)

Crest: On a rocky mount proper a dove rising proper holding in the
beak a slip of olive vert   Mantling: Gules and argent
For Philip Hamond, of Westacre High House, who m. 1803, Anne, dau.
of Charles James Packe, of Prestwold, Leics, and d. July 1824.
(B.L.G. 1937 ed.)

WICKMERE

1. All black background
Or on a fess between two chevrons sable three cross crosslets or
(Walpole)
Earl's coronet   Crest: The bust of a man in profile proper ducally
crowned or from which flows a long cap gules charged with a
catherine wheel or
Mantling: Gules and ermine   Supporters: Dexter, An antelope
argent: Sinister, A stag argent: both gorged with collars counter-
compony or and azure and chained or   Motto: Fari quae sentiat
Skull below
For Horace Walpole, 4th Earl of Orford, who d. unm. 2 Mar. 1797.
(B.P. 1949 ed.)
(There are three identical hatchments at Houghton)

2. All black background
Walpole, impaling, to the dexter, Sable a lion rampant argent, on a
canton argent a cross gules (Churchill), and to the sinister, Gules a
chevron between three combs argent (Tunstall)
Earl's coronet   Crest, mantling, motto and supporters: As 1.
For Horatio, 2nd Earl of Orford (2nd creation), who m. 1st, 1781,
Sophia, dau. of Charles Churchill, and 2nd, 1806, Catherine (née
Tunstall), widow of the Rev. Edward Chamberlayne, and d. 15 June
1822.   (B.P. 1949 ed.)

3. Dexter backbround black
Walpole, impaling, Paly of six argent and sable over all on a bend vert
three trefoils slipped or (Fawkener)
Earl's coronet   Crest, mantling, motto and supporters: As 1.
For Horatio, 3rd Earl of Orford, who m. 1812, Mary, dau. of William
Augustus Fawkener, of Brocton Hall, Salop, and d. 29 Dec. 1858.
(B.P. 1949 ed.)

4. Sinister background black
Qly, 1st and 4th, Walpole, 2nd and 3rd, Vert a lion rampant or
(Robsart)
In pretence: Argent three pallets gules within a bordure engrailed
azure on a canton gules a spur or (Knight)

Shield suspended from a bow of blue ribbon and flanked by palm
branches
For Elizabeth, dau. of Thomas Knight, of Downton Castle, who m.
Francis Walpole, and d. 3 Aug. 1860.   (B.P. 1949 ed.)

EAST WINCH

1. All black background
Sable three lions passant in bend between four bendlets argent (Browne)
Crest: An eagle displayed vert   Mantling: Gules and argent
A small hatchment, c. 2ft. x 2ft.
Unidentified

2. Exactly as 1, but very small, only about 1ft. x 1ft.
Unidentified

WOODRISING

1. All black background
Ermine on a cross gules five escallops or (Weyland)   In pretence:
Gules a fess between two chevrons argent (Nourse)
Crest: A lion rampant sable   Mantling: Gules and argent
Motto: Resurgam
For John Weyland, who m. 1772, Elizabeth Johanna, dau. and co-heir
of John Nourse, of Woodeaton, and d. 24 July 1825.   (B.L.G. 1937
ed.)
(There is an identical hatchment for John Weyland in the parish church
of Woodeaton, Oxfordshire)

2. Sinister background black
Weyland, impaling, Azure a talbot passant or, on a chief indented
argent three cross crosslets sable (Keene)
Mantling: Gules and argent   Motto: Resurgam   Cherub's head
above shield
For Elizabeth, dau. and heir of Whitstead Keene, of Richmond, who m.
John Weyland, and d. 30 Apr. 1845.   (B.L.G. 1937 ed.)
(There is an identical hatchment in the parish church at Scoulton, q.v.)

3. All black background
Arms: As 2.
Crest, mantling and motto: As 1.
For John Weyland, who d. 1854.   (B.L.G. 1937 ed.: H. Jaques)

4. All black background
Weyland, impaling, Azure three boars' heads erased close or a bordure
chequy or and azure (Gordon)

Crest, mantling and motto: As 1.
For Richard Weyland, who m. 1820, Charlotte, dau. of Charles Gordon
of Cluny, and d. Oct. 1864. (B.L.G. 1937 ed.)
(There is also a hatchment for Richard Weyland in the parish church of
Woodeaton, Oxfordshire)

WOODTON

1. All black background
Per pale gules and azure three bucks trippant or (Suckling), impaling,
Argent a fess gules between three choughs proper (Framlingham)
In pretence: Sable a ram or (Ramell)
Crest: A buck courant gules attired or   Motto: Mora trahit
periculum
For Maurice William Suckling, who m. 1st, Catherine Framlingham, of
Lynn, who d. 1814.   He m. 2nd, Caroline Ramell, and d.s.p. 1820.
She d. 1855.   (B.L.G. 1937 ed.)

2. All black background
On a lozenge   Or on a fess azure four crescents argent (Yelloly),
impaling, Qly, 1st and 4th, Or on a chevron azure between three mari-
golds slipped and leaved proper two lions respectant argent (Tyssen),
2nd and 3rd, Azure on a bend cotised or three griffins' heads erased
azure (Bodicote)
Mantling: Gules and argent.   Motto: Spes mea Christus
For Sarah, dau. of Samuel Tyssen of Narborough Hall, who m. Dr.
John Yelloly, M.D., F.R.S., and d. 21 Oct. 1854, aged 70.   (F. H.
Suckling, 'A Forgotten Past')

WORSTEAD

1. Dexter background black
Per pale azure and gules a cross engrailed ermine (Berney), impaling,
Per pale argent and or on a chief indented sable three lions rampant or
(Beevor)
Crest: A plume of five ostrich feathers alternately argent and azure
Mantling: Gules and argent   Motto: In coelo quies
For Robert Berney, who m. Charlotte (Beevor), and d. 28 Aug. 1828.
(Farrer)

2. Sinister background black
Argent three lions passant guardant in pale gules (Brograve)   In
pretence: Azure a hawk on a perch or (Hawker)
Crest: A double-headed eagle wings displayed and inverted ermine,
beaked, legged and ducally crowned or   Motto: Finis dat esse

For Jane, dau. of Edward Hawker, of Gt. Baddow, Essex, who m. as
his 1st wife, Sir Berney Brograve, Bt., and d. 6 Aug. 1765.
(Farrer;   'Complete Baronetage')

3. **Sinister background black**
Qly of eleven, 1st, Brograve, 2nd, Qly per fess indented gules and argent
in the 1st and 4th quarters a crescent argent in the 2nd and 3rd a
leopard's face gules (Ryton), 3rd, Argent two lions passant guardant
gules (Littlebury), 4th, Barry of eight gules and ermine (Kirton), 5th,
Argent a bend between six cross crosslets fitchy azure (Woodthorpe),
6th, Qly, i. and iv. Ermine, ii. and iii. chequy or and gules (Gibthorpe),
7th, Argent a chevron gules between three nails azure (St.

Cleere),
8th, Gules a griffin segreant or within a bordure engrailed argent
(Battell), 9th, Argent two chevronels between eleven billets, five and
six sable (Lelholme), 10th, Qly azure and gules a cross engrailed ermine
(Berney), 11th, Hawker, impaling, Fusilly gules and or a bordure azure
(Halcott)
Motto: Finis dat esse   Shield suspended from a lover's knot
Two cherubs' heads at top corners of shield
For Jane, dau. of Matthew Halcott, of Hoe, who m. 1769, as his second
wife, Sir Berney Brograve, Bt., and d. 14 May 1793.   (Farrer:
'Complete Baronetage')

4. **All black background**
Qly of twelve, 1st, Brograve, with Badge of Ulster, 2nd, Ryton, 3rd,
Littlebury, 4th, Kirton, 5th, Woodthorpe, 6th, Gibthorpe, 7th, St.
Cleere, 8th, Battell, 9th, Argent a chevron between ten billets, six and
four sable (Lelholme), 10th, Leventhorpe, 11th, Qly gules and azure a
cross engrailed ermine (Berney), 12th, Brograve   To dexter of main
shield, Brograve impaling Hawker, with S.Bl.   To sinister of main
shield, Brograve, with Badge of Ulster, and in pretence, Halcott, with
S.Bl.
Crest: As 2.   Mantling: Gules and argent   Motto: Finis dat esse
Two cherubs' heads at top corners of shield
For Sir Berney Brograve, Bt., who d. 1796 or 1797.   (Farrer;
'Complete Baronetage')

WYMONDHAM

1. **Dexter background black**
Argent two chevrons between three chaplets vert roses gules (Burroughes), impaling, Azure three quatrefoils argent (Vincent)   To
dexter of main shield, Burroughes, impaling, Gules on a cross argent
five molets pierced sable (Randall) A.Bl.   To sinister of main shield,
Burroughes, impaling, Vincent   D.Bl.

Crest: A griffin's head erased argent charged on the neck with two
chevrons vert   No mantling or motto
For Jeremiah Burroughes, of Wymondham, who m. 1st, Anne, dau. of
Thomas Randall.   She d. 10 Oct. 1734, aged 36.   He m. 2nd,
— Vincent, and d. 27 Nov. 1759.   (B.L.G. 1937 ed.)

2. Sinister background black
Burroughes   In pretence: Qly, 1st and 4th, Argent a fess azure
(Burkin), 2nd and 3rd, Qly gules and argent (Cock)
Crest: As 1.   Motto: In coelo quies
For Diana, dau, and co-heir of James Burkin of North Burlingham, who
m. Jeremiah Burroughes, of Wymondham, and d. 22 Dec. 1764.
(B.L.G. 1937 ed.)

3. All black background
Burroughes, with label of three points for difference   In pretence:
Burkin quartering Cock
Crest: As 1.   Motto: Spes mea in Deo
For Jeremiah Burroughes, who d. 7 Déc. 1767.   (B.L.G. 1937 ed.)

4. Dexter background black
Burroughes, with crescent for difference   In pretence: Argent two
bars gules in chief three cinquefoils sable (Denton)
Crest: As 1.   Mantling: Gules and argent   Motto: Resurgam
For Randall Burroughes, of Burfield Hall, Wymondham, who m. Anne,
dau. and co-heir of Samuel Denton, and d. 9 Sept. 1817.   (B.L.G.
1937 ed.)

5. All black background
On a lozenge   Arms: As 4.
Motto: Resurgam
For Anne, widow of Randall Burroughes.   She d. 30 Jan. 1827.
(B.L.G. 1937 ed.)

6. All black background
On a lozenge surmounted by a cherub's head
Qly, 1st and 4th, Burroughes, 2nd and 3rd, Denton
Mantling: Gules and argent
Unidentified
(These hatchments are now stored in the tower; in most instances vert
and azure has darkened to sable)

GREAT YARMOUTH, St. Nicholas

1. Dexter background black
Qly, 1st, Vert a fess embattled or between in chief two pheons and in
base two shinbones in saltire argent (Cooper), 2nd, Sable a saltire argent,

on a chief argent three bulls' heads cabossed with rings in their noses
sable (Lovick), 3rd, Argent on a bend cotised sable between two
fleurs-de-lys gules a lion passant or (Bransby), 4th, Argent six fleurs-de-
lys azure a chief indented or (Paston), impaling, Azure on a bend wavy
or three Cornish choughs proper a bordure engrailed argent charged
with four roundels gules and four roundels azure alternately (Rede)
Crest: From a mural crown argent the upper part of a spear erect
proper pointed and fringed or, surmounted by two palm branches in
saltire vert
Mantling: Gules and argent   Motto: Nil magnum nisi bonum
Skull below shield
For the Rev. Samuel Lovick Cooper, who m. 1787, Sarah Lemon, dau.
of Thomas Rede, of Beccles, and d. 3 July 1817, aged 64.   (Farrer)

2. **Dexter background black**
Shield and lozenge   Dexter, shield, within Order of the Bath, Qly,
1st, Gules on a chevron between three keys in pale or three fleurs-de-
lys sable (Parker), 2nd, Sable two bars engrailed or (Rouse), 3rd,
Chequy or and sable a fess gules fretty or (   ), 4th, Or a lion rampant
barry gules and sable (   )   Sinister, lozenge, within an ornamental
wreath, Qly, 1st and 4th, Gules a horse courant or a chief ermine (for
Butt), 2nd and 3rd, Or on a bend gules three doves or (   )
Crest: An elephant's head erased argent tusked or
Mantling: Gules and or   Motto: Try   Skull below
For Admiral Sir George Parker, K.C.B., who m. Arabella, dau. of Peter
Butt, and d. 1847.   (Farrer)

3. **All black background**
Exactly as 2.
For Arabella, widow of Admiral Sir George Parker, K.C.B.   She d.
1850.   (Farrer)

The following hatchments are privately owned and no longer in the
parishes to which they originally belonged.

1. **All black background**
Two shields   Dexter, Sable an estoile of eight points or between two
flaunches ermine, in centre chief the Badge of Ulster (Hobart)
Sinister, Argent a lion rampant gules between three pheons and a bordure engrailed sable (Egerton)
Crests: Dexter, A bull passant per pale sable and gules bezanty, in the
nose a ring or   Sinister, On a chapeau gules and ermine a lion rampant gules supporting an arrow gules pheoned and flighted sable
Frame decorated with skulls and crossbones
For Sir John Hobart, 2nd Bt., who m. 2nd, 1621, Frances, eldest dau.
of John, Earl of Bridgewater, and d.s.p.m. 20 Apr. 1647.   She d.
27 Nov. 1664. Perhaps used subsequently for his widow.
(B.P. 1949 ed.)

(In the possession of Mr. Bryan Hall, Banningham Old Rectory;
formerly in Blickling church until the restoration of 1878.)

2. Sinister background black
Vert a lion rampant or (Norton)   In pretence, and impaling, Gules
two lions passant in pale ermine crowned or (Felton)
Crest: A Moor's head affronté proper   Mantling: Gules and argent
Motto: Confide recte agens
For Frances, dau. of Sir Compton Felton, Bt., of Playford, Suffolk,
who m. Thomas Norton of Ixworth Abbey, Suffolk, and d.
He d. 1748
(Farrer's 'Portraits in Suffolk Houses', p. 236; Harvey's 'Suffolk Green
Books', No. XIII)
(In the possession of Mr. Bryan Hall; formerly in the private chapel at
Ixworth abbey)

3. All black background
Qly, 1st and 4th, Or on a chevron sable three unicorns' heads erased
argent (Holl of Heigham and Twyford), 2nd and 3rd, Vert a stag
statant within a tressure flory counter-flory or (Warde of Twyford)
Crest: A lion-dragon sejant sable gutty or   Mantling: Gules and
argent
For a descendant of Augustine Holl (d. 1736) and Catherine (d. 1747),
dau. of James Warde.   (M. J. Sayer)
(In the possession of Mr. M. J. Sayer, Sparham House, Norwich)

4. All black background
Ermine a chief qly or and gules (Peckham), impaling, Or a stag's head
cabossed gules (   )
Crest: An ostrich argent in its beak a horseshoe vert
Mantling: Gules and argent
Unidentified
(In the possession of Mr. Brookes, The Grange, Wroxham)

5. Sinister background black
Sable on a fess counter-embattled between three goats passant argent
three roundels sable (Cornwallis), impaling, Argent a chevron between
three tigers' heads erased sable langued gules (Hayes)
Crest: A lion's head erased or charged with a roundel sable
Mantling: Gules and argent   Motto: Sola nobilitat virtus
Reputed to be for Laura, dau. of William Hayes, 2nd wife of James,
5th Earl Cornwallis.   She d. 1840.   (B.E.P.)
(In the *Black Lion* Hotel, Little Walsingham)

6. Sinister background black

Qly, 1st, Argent a cross engrailed gules (Gurney), 2nd, Paly of six or
and azure (Gournay), 3rd, Chequy azure and or a crescent argent
charged with a cinquefoil sable for difference (De Warenne), 4th,
Azure a chevron in chief three crosses formy argent (Barclay), impaling,
Qly, 1st, Barclay, 2nd, Argent a fess wavy gules between three boars'
heads couped sable langued gules (Allardice), 3rd, Argent on a chief
sable three escallops or (Graham), 4th, Or a fess chequy argent and
azure in chief a chevron gules, all within a double tressure flory gules
(Stewart)
No frame
For Margaret, dau. of Robert Barclay, of Urie, co. Kincardine, who m.
1809, Hudson Gurney, of Keswick, Norfolk, and d. 16 Dec. 1855.
(B.L.G. 1937 ed.)
(In the possession of Mr. R. Q. Gurney, Bawdeswell Hall; formerly in
Intwood church)

7. All black background

Arms: As 1., but chequy or and azure, etc. for De Warenne
Crests: 1. On a chapeau gules and ermine a gurnet in pale head down-
wards proper   2. A wrestling collar or   Mantling: Gules and argent
Motto: Resurgam
No frame
For Hudson Gurney, who d. 9 Nov. 1864.   (B.L.G. 1937 ed.)
(In the possession of Mr. R. Q. Gurney, Bawdeswell Hall; formerly in
Intwood church)

SUFFOLK

by

Joan Corder, F.S.A.

Long Melford: For Thomas, 1st Viscount Savage, 1635

INTRODUCTION

Suffolk, with 306, probably comes second only to Kent in the number of hatchments remaining in the county. In 1952 an exhaustive survey was made by H. Hawes and E. K. Stephenson, printed in *Proceedings of the Suffolk Institute of Archaeology*, Vol. XXVI, pp. 208-13, during which a total of 311 examples were recorded (among them, however, eight memorial boards which are excluded from this volume). During the intervening 20 years, seven of these hatchments have been lost; three at Stanningfield, one at Kesgrave, one at Fornham St. Martin, one at Theberton and one at Ufford now in rags. To offset which losses, ten hatchments have been discovered: two at Carlton, one at Hemingstone, two at Yaxley, one at Shrubland Park (now in Stonham Aspall church), two at Wissington, one at Withersfield, and one at Sudbourne.

The earliest hatchment in Suffolk is that of Viscount Savage at Long Melford, 1635— the latest that of Sir Thomas Warner, Bart., at Thorpe Morieux, 1934; covering a span of almost exactly three centuries.

Several instances may be found of the hatchments of married persons being placed in different churches; those of Thomas Kerridge at Shelley and his wife Jane at Framlingham, and of William Crawford at Haughley and his wife Elizabeth Dorothie at Wetherden being cases in point; and while the hatchments of the two husbands of Harriet Richardson (Philip Hamond and John Oliver) are at Hawkedon, her own is at Long Melford. Hatchments of sisters are at Barsham and Charsfield (Charlotte and Henrietta Jane Anderson), two others at Long Melford (Elizabeth and Nancy Service); while more complex relationships may be followed through those of Thomas Farr of North Cove who married Georgiana, daughter of Sir Thomas Gooch of Benacre—their eldest daughter, Georgiana Farr, marrying the Rev. Thomas Sheriffe of Henstead.

Two hatchments for the same person are at Barham and Crowfield, those for Sir William Fowle-Middleton, 2nd Bart. Different arms for the same person appear at Bramfield, where the impaled quarterly coats of Barnes and Bestney are given for Mary Kerrison (wife of Reginald Rabett); which coats were those of her mother—her correct paternal coat of Kerrison being shown on her own hatchment. Incorrect arms are painted on two hatchments at Henley, the first where Henrietta Gould married the evidently non-armigerous Thomas Sleorgin and the coats are those of her parents; the second where Mary, daughter of William Snell, married as his first wife John Medows Theobald— whose arms and quarterings alone appear on her hatchment. A change in status is recorded on the hatchments of Sir William Fowle-Middleton, 1st Bart., and his wife Harriot Acton at Barham. Sir William's arms impale those of his wife on his hatchment, as was correct when he died in 1829— but, shortly after 1836, Harriot became an heiress by the deaths of her brother (*see* Stonham Aspall) and her elder sister; thus her arms were placed on an escutcheon of pretence on her hatchment when she died many years later. Divorce is noted in negative fashion on the hatchment of Bernard, 12th Duke of Norfolk at Fornham St. Martin—the arms of his former wife and the mother of his heir, Lady Elizabeth Belasyse, being completely omitted. Lady Elizabeth's sister, Lady Anne Belasyse, was more fortunate—her hatchment, as the first wife of Sir George Wombwell, Bart., hangs at Stowlangtoft. The Rev. Seymour Leeke of Yaxley chose also to ignore his wife, Mary Rant, from whom he was separated.

A rare example of supporters to a commoner is shown by the hatchment of Edmund Tyrell at Gipping: which supporters had been borne by this old family for generations. However, quite unauthorised robes form backdrops for the arms of William Shuldham at Marlesford and for those of Mrs. Eleanor Sharpe at Melton. An augmentation of honour, a canton of Austria, is borne on the arms of Sir Robert Pocklington at Chelsworth; whose hatchment also displays the Order of Maria Theresa awarded to him for gallantry in 1794—and supporters in the figures of British and Austrian cavalrymen, the latter presumably self-awarded.

The frames of many hatchments are of interest, particularly some of the earlier examples; for, among the variety of emblems of mortality to be found on them are skulls and bones at Framlingham, beautifully carved or appliquéd cherubs' heads and what appear to be interlaced vine leaves at Halesworth, winged hour-glasses and thigh bones at Boxted and winged skulls, branches of (probably) bay leaves and flowers and banks of cloud at Pakenham.

National heroes touch the hatchments of Suffolk; Lord Nelson's uncle, William Suckling, is remembered by his at Barsham, while that of Rebecca, eldest daughter of Clive of India, hangs in Denston church.

Joan Corder, F.S.A.
Felixstowe,
May 1973

ALDEBURGH

1. All black background
Qly, 1st and 4th, Argent a fret sable (Vernon), 2nd and 3rd, Argent on
a fess azure three garbs or (Vernon)
Crest: A boar's head erased sable ducally gorged or
Mantling: Gules and argent   Motto: Resurgam
For Leveson Vernon, who d. unm. 1831.   (B.L.G. 1853 ed.;
Copinger, V, 98)

AMPTON

1. Dexter background black
Per pale and per chevron, 1st, Chequy or and azure a fess ermine
(Calthorpe), 2nd, Ermine a maunch gules (Calthorpe ancient), 3rd,
Gules on a fess argent between three boars' heads couped or a lion
passant azure (Gough), in centre chief the Badge of Ulster   In
pretence: Paly of six argent and gules on a chevron azure three cross
crosslets or (Carpenter)
Baron's coronet   Crest: A boar's head couped at the neck azure,
bristled and tusked or, between two woodmen with clubs over their
shoulders and wreathed about the temples and loins with leaves, all
proper
Motto: Resurgam   Supporters: Two woodmen as in the crest
For Henry, 1st Baron Calthorpe, who m. Frances, 2nd dau. and co-heir
of Gen. Benjamin Carpenter, and d. 16 Mar. 1798.   (B.P. 1949 ed.)

2. All black background
On a lozenge   Per pale and per chevron, 1st, Chequy or and azure a
fess ermine (Calthorpe), 2nd, Argent a maunch gules (Calthorpe
Ancient), 3rd, Gules on a fess argent between three boars' heads couped
or a lion passant gules (Gough)
In pretence: Argent three pallets gules on a chevron azure three cross
crosslets or (Carpenter)
Baroness's coronet   Mantle: Gules and ermine   Supporters: As 1.
For Frances, widow of Henry, 1st Baron Calthorpe.   She d. 1 May
1827.   (B.P. 1949 ed.)

GREAT ASHFIELD

1. Dexter background black
Qly, 1st and 4th, Argent on a chevron between two chevronels sable
three portcullises argent (Thurlow), 2nd and 3rd, Sable a cross or
charged with a crescent sable for difference (Hovell), impaling, Sable

a hawk close argent beaked, legged and belled or, on a canton or a
lozenge gules (Bolton)
Baron's coronet   Crest: A greyhound couchant or collared and lined
sable
Motto: Quo fata vocant   Supporters: Two greyhounds or collared
and lined sable
For Edward, 2nd Baron Thurlow, who m. Mary Katherine, dau. of
James Richard Bolton, and d. 3 June 1829.   (B.P. 1891 ed.)

2. Sinister background black
Qly, as 1., impaling, Per chevron engrailed or and azure three martlets
counterchanged (Hodgson)
Baroness's coronet   Supporters: As 1.
For Sarah, only dau. of Peter Hodgson, who m. Edward Thomas, 3rd
Baron Thurlow, and d. 13 Mar. 1840.   (B.P. 1949 ed.)

3. All black background
Arms, as 2., but without crescent for difference
Baron's coronet   Crest: As 1.   Mantling: Gules and argent
Motto: Fides   Supporters: As 1.
For Edward Thomas, 3rd Baron Thurlow, who d. 2 Mar. 1857.
(B.P. 1949 ed.)

4. All black background
Arms, as 3., but no impalement
Baron's coronet   Crest, motto and supporters: As 1.
For Edward, 4th Baron Thurlow, who d. unm. 22 Apr. 1874.
(B.P. 1949 ed.)

5. All black background
Qly, 1st, Sable a hawk close argent belled or (Bolton of Bolton,
Lancs), 2nd, Gules three bird bolts or (Bolton of Yorks), 3rd, Gules
three wolves' heads erased or (Bolton of Suffolk), 4th, Sable a chevron
between three molets pierced or (? Mansell), impaling, Azure three
fleurs-de-lys or (   )
Crest: A hawk close argent belled or   Motto: Un dieu un roy une
foy
Probably for James Richard Bolton, who d.
(B.P. 1891 ed.)

ASPALL

1. Dexter background black
Argent on a cross gules five escallops or (Chevallier), impaling, Chequy
argent and sable on a pale argent three molets gules (Fiske)
Crest: A lion's head erased argent
For the Rev. Temple Chevallier, who m. Mary, dau. of the Rev. Thomas
Fiske, and d. 24 Aug. 1804.   (B.L.G. 1937 ed.)

2. **All black background**
On a lozenge   Argent on a cross gules five escallops argent (Chevallier), impaling, Chequy argent and sable on a pale argent three molets pierced gules (Fiske)
Lozenge surmounted by a cherub's head
For Mary, widow of the Rev. Temple Chevallier.   She d. 7 Nov. 1807.
(Top. and Gen. II, 159)

BARDWELL

1. **Dexter background black**
Qly, 1st and 4th, Gules on a bend argent three shovellers close sable, beaked and legged gules (Reade), 2nd, Or three bulls heads couped sable, in chief a crescent sable for difference (Crofts), 3rd, Gules a chevron engrailed between three owls argent (Hewitt)   In pretence: Gules an eagle displayed and a chief or (Harrison)
Crest: A shoveller close sable, beaked and legged gules
Mantling: Gules and argent   Frame decorated with skulls, crossbones and hourglasses
For Charles Crofts Reade, elder son of Sir Charles Crofts Reade, and Mary, dau. of Sir Thos. Hewitt.   He m. 1698, Susan, dau. of James Harrison, of co. Cambs, and d. 1720.   She d. 1745.   (Farrer MS.: Lincs. Peds. Harl. Soc., p. 816)

BARHAM

1. **Dexter background black**
Argent fretty sable on a canton sable a unicorn's head erased or in chief the Badge of Ulster (Middleton), impaling, Gules a fess engrailed within a bordure engrailed ermine (Acton)
Crest: A garb or banded vert between two wings sable
Mantle: Gules and argent   Motto: Regardez mon droit
For Sir William Fowle Middleton, 1st Bt., who m. Harriot, dau. of Nathaniel Lee Acton, of Bramford Hall, and d. 26 Dec. 1829;
(Debrett's 'Baronetage', 1828; Copinger, II, 244; E.A. N. and Q., VI, 180-1)

2. **All black background**
On a lozenge   Qly, 1st and 4th, Argent fretty sable on a canton per chevron or and sable a unicorn's head erased per chevron gules and or horned sable (Middleton), 2nd and 3rd, Argent a chevron gules on a chief gules three molets argent (Fowle), in chief the Badge of Ulster
In pretence: Qly, 1st and 4th, Ermine a fess within a bordure gules (Acton), 2nd and 3rd, Argent a chevron between in chief two roundels and in base a martlet sable (Lee)

Motto: Resurgam
For Harriot, widow of Sir William Fowle Middleton, 1st Bt.   She d.
25 Aug. 1852, aged 98.   (Copinger, I, 129; E.A. N. and Q., VI, 36,
180-1)

3. Dexter background black
Qly, 1st, Argent fretty sable on a canton per chevron sable and or a
unicorn's head erased per chevron or and gules (Middleton), 2nd,
Fowle, as 2., 3rd, Gules a fess engrailed within a bordure ermine
(Acton), 4th, Or a chevron between in chief two roundels and in base a
martlet sable (Lee), over all the Badge of Ulster, impaling, Qly, 1st and
4th, Ermine on a chevron sable three fountains proper (Cust), 2nd and
3rd, Or an inescutcheon within a orle of martlets sable (Brownlow)
Crests: Dexter, A garb or banded vert between two wings sable
(Middleton) Sinister, A griffin's head erased argent pierced through the
neck with an arrow or (Fowle)   Mantling: Gules and argent
Motto: Regardez mon droit
For Sir William Fowle Fowle Middleton, 2nd Bt., who m. Hon. Anne
Cust, dau. of Lord Brownlow, and d. 2 May, 1860.   (E.A. N. and Q.
VI, 36, 181)
(There is an identical hatchment at Crowfield, q.v.)

4. All black background
On a lozenge   Qly, 1st Argent fretty sable on a canton per fess sable
and gules a unicorn's head erased or in base (Middleton), 2nd Fowle,
3rd, Acton, as 1., 4th, Lee, the field or, over all the Badge of Ulster,
impaling, Qly, 1st and 4th, Cust, 2nd and 3rd, Brownlow
For Anne, widow of Sir William Fowle Fowle Middleton, 2nd Bt.
She d. 8 May 1867.   (E.A. N. and Q. VI, 181)

5. Dexter background black
Qly, 1st and 4th, qly i. Middleton, as 1., ii. Fowle, iii. Gules a fess
engrailed within a bordure engrailed ermine (Acton), iv. Lee, the field
argent, 2nd and 3rd, qly, i. Or a cross engrailed per pale gules and
sable (Broke), ii. Argent a chevron between three stags' heads cabossed
sable (Parker), iii. Ermine three longbows paleways in fess gules on a
chief azure three leopards' faces or (Bowes), iv. Azure semy-de-lys and
a lion rampant or (Beaumont), over all the Badge of Ulster, impaling,
Qly, 1st and 4th, Argent a chevron between three boars' heads couped
close sable (Evans), 2nd and 3rd, Sable an antelope salient argent
(Harris)
Order of the Bath suspended below shield
Crests: 1. A garb or banded vert between two wings sable (Middleton)
2. From a naval coronet or a dexter arm embowed encircled with a
wreath of laurel proper and holding a trident or (Broke Augmentation)

3. Fowle, the griffin's head sable   Motto: Saevumque tridentem ser-
vamus
For Sir George Nathaniel Broke-Middleton, 3rd Bt. who m. Albinia
Maria, dau. of Thomas Evans, of Lyminster, and d. 1887.
(Copinger, I, 129)

BARKING

1. **Dexter background black**
Gules a fess between six molets argent (Ashburnham), impaling Azure a
moon in her complement between nine estoiles, three, two, three, one
argent (Baillie)
Earl's coronet   Crest: From a ducal coronet or an ash tree proper
Supporters: Two greyhounds sable lined and collared or
Motto: Le roy et l'estat
For Bertram, 4th Earl of Ashburnham, of Barking Hall, who m.
Katharine Charlotte, dau. of George Baillie, of Jerviswood, co. Lanark,
and d. 22 June 1878.   (B.P; 1891 ed.)
(There is an identical hatchment in the parish church at Ashburnham,
Sussex)

BARSHAM

1. **Dexter background black**
Qly of six, 1st, Azure on a bend wavy or three martlets proper, all
within a bordure argent charged with roundels gules and azure (Rede),
2nd, Argent three wings conjoined in lure bendwise gules between
double cotises sable (for Wingfield), 3rd, Argent a fess sable between
three whales naiant proper (Leman), 4th, Qly or and gules (? Bovill),,
5th, Sable three martlets proper (Naunton), 6th, Per fess indented azure
and argent (Glanville), impaling, Argent a chevron between three
crosses patonce sable (Anderson)
Crest: A stag's head argent attired and collared or between tufts of grass
or
Mantling: Gules and argent   Motto: Εφυγον .a.ον ευρον αμεινον
Skull and crossbones in base
For Robert Rede, who m. Charlotte, dau. of Sir William Anderson, Bt.,
and d. 13 Aug. 1822.   (B.L.G. 1853 ed.: Suckling, I, 30)

2. **All black background**
On a lozenge   Arms: As 1.
Mantling: Gules and argent   Motto: Christus mea vita   Cherub's
head above
For Charlotte, widow of Robert Rede.   She d. 9 Oct. 1822.
(B.L.G. 1853 ed: Suckling; Debrett's 'Baronetage' 1828)

3. **Dexter background black**
Azure on a bend wavy or three choughs proper within a bordure
engrailed argent charged with roundels gules and sable (Rede)
In pretence: Argent a chevron between three heronshaws sable
(Henshaw)
Crest: A stag's head sable attired and charged on the neck with a bar
gemel or, between branches vert   Mantling: Gules and argent
Motto: Resurgam
On a square shield
For Robert Rede, formerly Cooper, who m. Louisa, dau, and co-heir
of Benjamin Henshaw, of Moor Hall, Essex, and d. before 1855.
(B.L.G. 1853 ed; Suckling)

4. **Dexter background black**
Per pale azure and gules three stags trippant or in chief a crescent argent
for difference (Suckling), impaling, Qly, 1st and 4th, Azure a cinquefoil
within a bordure ermine (Rumsey), 2nd and 3rd, Argent a fess gules in
chief a label of three points azure (Rumsey)
Crest: A stag courant or in its mouth a sprig of honeysuckle proper
Mantling: Gules and argent   Motto: Mors janua vitae
Two cherubs' heads at top of shield and skull at base
For William Suckling, of Banham Haugh, Norfolk, Comptroller of the
Customs, who m. Mary, dau. of Thomas Rumsey, of Kentish Town, and
d. 1798.   (Suckling I, 40, B.L.G. 1900 ed.)

BECCLES

1. **All black background**
Argent a fess between three cross crosslets fitchy gules (Crane)
Crest: A crane proper   Mantling: Gules and argent
Frame dated 1691
Probably for William Crane, gent., of Beccles, who m. Sarah – , and
had two daughters baptised at Beccles 1645/6 and 1652.   (Howard,
'Visit. of Suff.' 1561, I, 159)

2. **All black background**
Argent a lion rampant guardant sable between three crescents gules
(Brownrigg), impaling, Qly, 1st and 4th, Gules three dragons passant
in pale or (Blosse), 2nd and 3rd, Gules a saltire argent (Cage)
Crest: A lion statant guardant per pale gules and argent
Mantling: Gules and argent
R.B. in gold letters at top and the date 1669 below
For Robert Brownrigg, Barrister and J.P., who m. Mary, dau. of
Thomas Blosse of Belstead and his 1st wife, Mary, heir of Will. Cage of
Ipswich. He d. 1669.('Visit. of Suff.' 1664-8; E.A. Misc. 1921, 65)

BEDINGFIELD

1. Dexter background black
Ermine an eagle displayed gules beaked and legged or (Bedingfield),
impaling, Argent a chevron gules between three lions' heads erased
sable (Piersy)
Crest: A demi-eagle displayed gules
Mantling: Gules and argent   Motto: Despicio terrena
Skull and crossbones in base
For John James Bedingfield, who m. 1800, Sarah, dau. and co-heir of
Paul Piersy, of Fairhill, co. Cork, and d. 7 Jan. 1853.   (Farrer MS., I,
516; church window)

BENACRE

1. All black background
Per pale argent and sable a chevron between three talbots passant all
counterchanged, on a chief gules three leopards' faces or, in chief the
Badge of Ulster (Gooch)   In pretence: Sable a bend argent (   ),
impaling, Gules a fess between three roundels argent (   )
Crest: A talbot passant per pale argent and sable
Mantling: Gules and argent   Motto: Fide et virtute   Skull below
Unidentified

2. Dexter background black
Gooch, impaling, Sable a fess between three mascles argent (Whittaker),
the Badge of Ulster in centre chief, over line of impalement
Crest, mantling and motto: As 1.
For Sir Thomas Sherlock Gooch, 5th Bt., who m. Marianne, dau. of
Abraham Whittaker, of Lyston House, co. Hereford, and d. 18 Dec.
1851.   (B.P. 1953 ed.; Suckling II, 125)

3. Sinister background black
Gooch, in centre chief the Badge of Ulster   In pretence: Qly, 1st and
4th, Argent on a pale gules three crescents argent (Hayward), 2nd and
3rd, Ermine fretty sable, on a chief sable three fleurs-de-lys argent
(Patten)
Mantling: Gules and argent   Motto: In coelo quies
Cherubs' heads above shield
For Anna Maria, dau. and heir of William Hayward of Weybridge
(descended from family of Patten, of Bank), who m. Sir Thomas
Gooch, 4th Bt., and d. 28 Sept. 1814, aged 72.   (B.P. 1953 ed.;
Suckling, II 125)

4. Sinister background black
Gooch (talbots statant), in chief the Badge of Ulster   In pretence:

Qly, 1st and 4th, Gules a lion rampant argent between eight acorns or (Atwood), 2nd and 3rd, Argent three battle axes sable (? Gibbs)
Motto: In coelo quies   Two cherubs' heads at top of shield and skull in base
For Anne, dau. and heir of John Atwood, of Yarmouth, who m. as his 1st wife, Sir Thomas Gooch, 3rd Bt., and d. 1 Apr. 1767, aged 45.
(B.P. 1953 ed; Suckling, II, 125; Betham's 'Baronetage', III, 239-40)

5. All black background
Gooch, at fess point the Badge of Ulster, impaling, Sable
Crest, mantling and motto: As 1.
Unidentified

6. Dexter and top sinister background black
Gooch, at fess point the Badge of Ulster, impaling, two coats per fess;
1, Sable a chevron between three owls argent (Prescott) 2, Argent on a fess azure three molets argent (Vere)
Crest: As 1.but talbot argent   Mantling and motto: As 1.
For Sir Edward Sherlock Gooch, 6th Bt., who m. 1st, Louisa Anna Maria, dau. of Sir George Beeston Prescott, Bt.   She d. 24 Feb. 1837 or 1838.   He m. 2nd, Harriet, dau. of James Hope Vere, and d. 9 Nov. 1856.   (B.P. 1953 ed.; Suckling, II, 125)

7. Dexter background black
Gooch, in chief the Badge of Ulster
Crest and motto: As 1.   Mantling: Sable and argent
Unidentified

8. Dexter background black
Gooch (talbots statant), in chief the Badge of Ulster
Crest: As 1., but talbots statant   Mantling and motto: as 7.
Unidentified

BENHALL

1. Sinister background black
On a lozenge   Azure semy of trefoils slipped and a lion rampant argent (Hollond), impaling, Vert on a chevron between three harts trippant or semy of roundels sable three quatrefoils gules (Robinson)
Motto: Resurgam
For Isabella Esther, dau. of the Rev. Sir John Robinson, 1st Bt., of Rokeby Hall, co. Louth, Ireland, who m. 1839, the Rev. Edmund Hollond, of Benhall Lodge, and d. 23 Jan. 1848.   (B.L.G. 1871 ed; B.P. 1868 ed.)

BOXTED

1. Dexter background black
Qly, 1st and 4th, Or a lion rampant sable (Poley), 2nd and 3rd, Sable
two chevronels between three roses argent (Weller), impaling, Qly, 1st
and 4th, Or a cross vert (Hussey), 2nd and 3rd, Sable a bend between
six cross crosslets fitchy argent (Lake)
Crest: A lion rampant sable collared and chained or
Mantling: Gules and argent   Motto: Fortior qui se (vincit)
Frame inscribed 'G. W. Poley. Died. Decr. 29 1778'
For George Weller Poley, son of Robert Weller, of Tunbridge, and his
wife Elizabeth Poley. He m. Frances, dau. of Thomas Hussey, of Bur-
wash, Sussex, and d. 29 Dec. 1778.   (B.L.G. 1853 ed. and inscr. on
hatchment)

2. All white background
Qly of five, 1st and 4th, Poley, 2nd and 3rd, Weller, 5th, (to sinister)
Lake
Crest, mantling and motto: As 1.
Frame inscribed 'G. W. Poley. Died April 10 1780'
For George Weller Poley, eldest son of George Weller Poley.   He d.
unm. 10 Apr. 1780.   (B.L.G. 1900 ed. and inscr. on hatchment)

3. Dexter background black
Poley, impaling, Argent on a chevron between three whales' heads
erased sable three wings argent (Whaley)
Crest: As 1.
Frame inscribed 'Rev. J. W. Poley. Died May 29 1799'
For the Rev. John Weller Poley, second son and afterwards heir of
George Weller Poley, who m. Jane, dau. of John Blatch Whaley, of
Colchester, and d. 29 May 1799.   (B.L.G. 1853 ed. and inscr. on
hatchment)

4. All black background
On a lozenge   Poley, impaling, Whaley
Motto: Resurgam   Escallop shell above
Frame inscribed 'Mrs Poley. Died Decr. 20 1833'
For Jane, widow of the Rev. John Weller Poley.   She d. 20 Dec. 1833.
(B.L.G. 1853 ed. and inscr. on hatchment)

5. All black background
Poley
Crest and mantling: As 1.   Motto: Resurgam
Frame inscribed 'Rev. W. W. Poley. died Feb. 1837'
For the Rev. William Weller Poley, who d. unm. Feb. 1837, aged 72.
(B.L.G. 1853 ed.)

6. Dexter background black
Poley, impaling, Gules three demi-lions and a chief or (Fisher)
Crest and mantling: As 1.   Motto: In coelo quies
Frame inscribed 'George Weller Poley. Died Nov. 5 1849'
For George Weller Poley, who m. Helen Sophia, dau. of James Fisher of
Browston Hall, and d. 5 Nov. 1849.   (B.L.G. 1900 ed.)

7. All black background
Poley
Crest, mantling and motto: As 1.
Frame decorated with emblems of mortality
Possibly for Robert, son of George Weller Poley.   He d. 1756.
(Farrer: 'Portraits in West Suffolk Houses', 38)

BRAMFIELD

1. Sinister background black
Argent a chevron sable gutty or between three rabbits' heads couped
sable (Rabett)   In pretence: Per chevron or and gules three lions
passant counterchanged (Lund)
Mantling: Gules and argent   Motto: In coelo quies   Shell-like
cartouche above
For Elizabeth, wife of Reginald Rabett, of Bramfield Hall.   She d.
15 July 1760, aged 68.   (Mills MS.: B.L.G. 1853 ed.: Top. et Gen. I,
475)

2. All black background
Rabett, as 1.   In pretence: Lund
Crest: A demi-rabbit rampant sable gutty or
Motto: Mors janua vitae
For Reginald Rabett, of Bramfield Hall, High Sheriff of Suffolk, 1737,
m. Elizabeth, and d. 25 Jan. 1763, aged 70.   (Sources, as 1.)

3. Dexter background black
Argent a chevron sable gutty argent between three rabbits' heads
couped sable (Rabett), impaling, Qly, 1st and 4th, Argent two bars
raguly sable and in chief three roundels gules (Barnes), 2nd and 3rd,
Per pale sable and gules a lion rampant guardant argent crowned or
(Bestney)
Crest: A demi-rabbit rampant sable.   Mantling: Gules and argent
Motto: In coelo quies   Skull and two wings below
For Reginald Rabett, who m. Mary, dau, of Matthias Kerrison, of
Bungay, and Mary Barnes.   He d. 31 May 1810, aged 39.
(Sources, as 1.)

4. All black background
On a lozenge surmounted by a cherub's head
Rabett, as 1., impaling, Or on a pile azure three caltraps or (Kerrison)
Motto: Resurgam
For Mary, only dau. of Matthias Kerrison of Bungay, who m. 1st,
1792, Reginald Rabett, who d. 1810, and 2nd, Lieut. Garbett, R.N.,
and was bur. at Bramfield, 13 Mar. 1832.   (Sources, as 1.)

BREDFIELD

1. Dexter background black
Qly, 1st and 4th, Ermine a bend gules (Jenney), 2nd and 3rd, Gules a
chevron or between three leopards' faces cabossed argent (Edgar
ancient), impaling, Qly per fess indented or and azure a bend gules
(Langley)
Crest: On a glove lying fessways a hawk, all proper
Mantling: Gules and argent   Motto: Mors janua vitae
For Arthur Jenney of Rendlesham, who m. Mary Langley, and d.
1742.
(Burke's 'Commoners', III, 448)

2. All black background
Ermine a bend gules cotised or (Jenney), impaling, Edgar ancient
Crest, mantling and motto: As 1.
For Arthur Jenney, who m. 1711, Mirabella, seventh dau. of Henry
Edgar of Eye, widow of Robert Burley of Wisbech, and d. 1729.
She d. 1724.
(B.L.G. 1853 ed.; Aedes Edgarorum, 63)

BRENT ELEIGH

1. Dexter background black
Gules a chevron between three fleurs-de-lys or (Brown), impaling,
Argent fretty azure, over all a lion rampant gules (Goate)   In chief a
crescent or (over impalement line)
Crest: A lion rampant proper in his paw a fleur-de-lys or
Mantling: Gules and argent   Motto: Resurgam
For Dr. Thomas Brown, M.D., of Lostock Place, who m. Sarah
Dionesse, dau. of Edward Goate (from whom she inherited Brent
Eleigh manor), and d. 9 Sept. 1852, aged 77.   His widow d. 1866.
(Copinger, I, 42)

2. All black background
Sable on a pale rayonny argent a lion rampant or (Colman)
Crest: A caltrap or between two wings argent

Mantling: Gules, azure and or   On motto scroll: Brent Ely
Unidentified
(This hatchment is badly painted and in poor condition)

BRIGHTWELL

1. All black background

Qly, 1st, Azure a fess dancetty ermine between six cross crosslets
argent (Barnardiston), 2nd, Argent a lion rampant tail forked gules
(Havering), 3rd, Vert a saltire engrailed or (Franke), 4th, Sable three
combs argent (Tunstall), over all the Badge of Ulster   To dexter of
main shield, Barnardiston, with B. of U., impaling, Azure two swords in
saltire points upwards argent hilts and pommels or within a bordure
engrailed or (Brand) A.Bl.   To sinister of main sheld, Barnardiston,
with B. of U., impaling, Or two chevrons engrailed and a canton gules
charged with a mascle or (Reynardson) D.Bl.
Crest: A bittern or among rushes proper
Mantling: Gules and argent   Motto: Je trove bien
For Sir Samuel Barnardiston, 1st Bt., who m. 1st, Thomasine, dau. of
Joseph Brand, of Edwardstone, and 2nd, Mary, dau. of Sir Abraham
Reynardson, and d.s.p. 8 Nov. 1707, aged 88.   (B.E.B.; Leslie
Dow; Mills MS.)

2. Dexter background black

Qly, 1st and 4th, Barnardiston, 2nd, Havering, 3rd, Or two bars azure
between six martlets, three, two, one gules (Paynell), impaling,
Gyronny of eight or and sable on a canton azure a molet or (Blackerby)
Crest and mantling: As 1.   Motto: Pestis patriae pigrities
For Samuel Barnardiston of London, who succeeded to the Brightwell
estate in 1712, and who m. Anne, dau. of Samuel Blackerby, of Gray's
Inn, and d. 7 Oct. 1725.   (Sources, as 1.)

3. Sinister background black

Barnardiston, impaling, Gules a lion rampant reguardant or (Morrice)
Motto: Ad Deum qui dedit   Skull above shield
For Ann, dau. and co-heir of John Morrice, of Quendon, Essex, who m.
as his 1st wife, Arthur Barnardiston, and d. 19 Aug. 1731, aged 24.
(B.E.B.; 'Kedington and the Barnardistons',20; Dow. Mills MS.)

4. All black background

Barnardiston
To dexter of main shield, Barnardiston, impaling, Morrice   A.Bl.
To sinister of main shield, Barnardiston, impaling, Azure a chevron
between three griffins' heads erased argent, on a chief or a lion passant
between two roundels gules (Jennens)   D.Bl.

.

Crest and mantling: As 1.   Motto: In coelo quies   Skull in base
For Arthur Barnardiston, who m. 1st, Ann, dau. of John Morrice, and
2nd, Mary, dau. of Richard Jennens, of Warwickshire, and d. 3 Apr.
1737, aged 52.   (B.E.B.; Dow; Mills MS.)

BURY ST. EDMUNDS (Moyses Hall)

1. All black background
On a lozenge   Two coats per fess, in chief, Argent a chevron between
three mascles gules (Spring), in base, Argent a saltire gules (Gage), on
each coat the Badge of Ulster, and both impaling, Sable a crescent
between two molets in pale argent (Jermyn)   In pretence: Jermyn
Skull above lozenge   Frame decorated with skulls and crossbones
For Merelina, youngest dau. and co-heir of Thomas, Lord Jermyn, who
m. 1st, 1691, Sir Thomas Spring, 3rd Bt. of Pakenham, and 2nd, Sir
William Gage, 2nd Bt. of Hengrave Hall.   She d. 29 Aug. 1727, aged
52.   (B.E.B.; Gage's 'Thingoe', 204; Rushbrook Par. Regs. per Suff.
Green Books)

2. All black background
Qly, 1st and 4th, Spring, 2nd and 3rd, Jermyn, over all the Badge of
Ulster
Crest: A stag's head couped proper attired or
Mantling: Gules and argent   Motto: Non mihi sed patriae
For Sir William Spring, 4th Bt., d. unm. 1736, aged 40.   Buried at
Pakenham, 22 Mar. 1736.   (Howard, 'Vis. of Suff. 1561', I, 200;
Rushbrook and Pakenham Regs.)

BURY ST. EDMUNDS

The following two hatchments were reported in September 1968 as
being in the garage of an empty house. No further information has been
received since.

1. All black background
Qly, 1st and 4th, Qly per fess indented gules and or (Bromley), 2nd,
Gules on a chief indented or three escallops gules (Barrett), 3rd, Or a
bend engrailed between six roses gules (Warner)
Crest: A cock pheasant proper   Mantling: Gules and argent
Motto: Resurgam
Possibly for Nathaniel Warner Bromley, of Badmondisfield Hall in
Wickambrook (son of Wm. Bromley and his wife, Elizabeth Barrett),
who d. 8 Apr. 1844, aged 87.   His wife, Sarah Wright, d. 1808.
(Howard and Crisp, 'Visitation of England and Wales', Notes VI, 45)

2. All black background

On a lozenge surmounted by a cherub's head
Gules on a chief indented argent three escallops sable (Barrett), impaling, Argent a cross flory between four martlets sable (Byrd)
Skull below
For Sarah Byrd, who m. Nathaniel Barrett, of Badmondisfield Hall,
and d. 11 Oct. 1796, aged 68.   (E. Anglian Misc. 1923, p. 60;
Copinger, V, 302-3)

CARLTON-next-KELSALE

1. Dexter background black

Argent a chevron between three greyhounds' heads erased gules
(Fuller), impaling, Azure two lions rampant combatant or (Carter)
Crest: A greyhound's head erased gules   Mantling: Gules and argent
Motto: In coelo quies
For Osborne Fuller, who m. Harriet Carter, and was buried at Carlton
4 Sept. 1794, aged 83.
(Crisp, 'Regs. of Carlton', 59)

2. All black background

Arms, as 1, but on lozenge, surmounted by a cherub's head
Motto: Resurgam
For Harriet, widow of Osborne Fuller.   She was buried 3 Aug. 1803,
aged 50.   (Crisp, 'Regs. of Carlton', 59)

CHARSFIELD

1. Dexter background black

Two qly coats on dexter   In chief, Qly, 1st and 4th, Azure a fess
between three dolphins embowed argent (Leman), 2nd and 3rd, Argent
a fess between three crescents each containing a fleur-de-lys gules
(Orgill) In base, Qly, 1st and 4th, Azure a cross formy between four
molets or (Sterling), 2nd and 3rd, Sable three martlets argent (Naunton), all impaling, Argent a chevron between three crosses patonce
sable (Anderson)
Crests: Dexter, In a lemon tree leaved and fructed proper a pelican
argent feeding her young in a nest proper (Leman)   Sinister, A bull's
head erased sable armed or gorged with a garland proper (Orgill)
Mantling: Gules and argent   Motto: Volens semperque juvare paratus
For the Rev. Naunton Thomas Orgill, who assumed name and arms of
Leman by licence, 1808, and m. Henrietta Jane, dau. of the Rev. Sir
William Anderson, Bt., of Lea, co. Lincs, and d. 31 Jan. 1837.
(Suckling, II, 184)

2. All black background
Arms, as 1., but on lozenge surmounted by a cherub's head
Mantling: Gules and argent   Motto: In coelo quies
For Henrietta Jane, widow of the Rev. Naunton Thomas Orgill Leman.
She d. 9 Mar. 1843.   (Suckling, II, 184)

CHELSWORTH

1. Dexter background black
Paly of six argent and gules a bend counterchanged (Pocklington)
impaling, Argent a wolf rampant azure (Wood)
Crest: A swan close proper   Mantling: Gules and argent
Motto: Viret post funera virtus   Cherubs' heads at top corners of
shield and skull below
For Robert Pocklington, sergeant-at-law, who m. Sarah Wood, and
d. 1767.   (Pocklington's 'Chelsworth', 30, 58)

2. Sinister background black
Pocklington, with Pocklington in pretence:
Crest, mantling and motto: As 1.
Cherubs' heads at top corners of shield and skull below
For Pleasance Pykarell, later Pocklington, cousin and heir of Robert
Pocklington (No. 1), who m. Samuel Pocklington (née Sharpe) and
d. 1774.
(B.L.G. 1900 ed.; Pocklington's 'Chelsworth', 31, 59)

3. Dexter background black
Pocklington, with Augmentation of Honour, on a canton argent a
double-headed eagle displayed sable holding in his dexter claw a sceptre
and in his sinister an orb proper, impaling, Or on a bend sable three
legs in armour proper, the kneecaps or (Blagrave)
Crest and mantling: As 1.   Motto: Honor virtutis praemium
Supporters: Two Hussars proper, the dexter Austrian, the sinister
British
From the shield is pendant the ribbon and the badge of the Austrian
Order of Maria Theresa
For Sir Robert Pocklington, son and heir of 2., who m. Catherine, dau.
of John Blagrave, of Calcot Park, Reading, and d. 20 Sept. 1840,
aged 69.
(B.L.G. 1900 ed.)

CLARE

1. Dexter background black
Argent three bears' heads erased sable muzzled or, a chief gules

(Barker), impaling, Azure a maunch or, over all a bend paly of six
ermine and gules (Conyers)
Crest: A bear's head sable muzzled or   Mantling: Gules and argent
Motto: Resurgam (only R visible, other letters obscured by woodwork)
For Lt.-Colonel John Barker, of Clare Priory, who m. Caroline, dau. of
John Conyers of Copped Hall, Essex, and d. 27 Nov. 1804, aged 54.
(B.L.G. 1853, ed.: Proc. S.I.A., VIII, 232)

2. All black background
On a lozenge surmounted by a cherub's head
Arms, as 1, but bend of Conyers, Gules two pallets ermine
Motto: In coelo quies
For Caroline, widow of Lt.-Colonel John Barker.   She d. 8 Jan. 1848,
aged 79.   (Sources, as 1)

CODDENHAM

1. Sinister background black
Gules on a chief argent two molets pierced sable (Bacon)   In
pretence: Qly, 1st and 4th, Or an eagle displayed sable (Mercia), 2nd
and 3rd, Argent two bars sable each charged with three martlets or
(Temple)
Crest: A boar passant ermine   Mantling: Gules and argent
Motto: In coelo quies   Skull in base
For Dorothy, dau. and co-heir of Peter Temple, only son of Sir William
Temple, Bt., of Sheen, who m. Nicholas Bacon, of Shrubland Park, and
was buried 8 July 1758.   (Rix, 'Diary of Edmund Bohun', 2;
Copinger, II, 244)

2. All black background
Arms, crest, mantling and motto: As 1. but crescent gules at fess
point of shield in pretence
Skull in base
For Nicholas Bacon, of Shrubland Park, who m. Dorothy, dau. and
co-heir of Peter Temple, and d. 1767.   (Sources, as 1)

3. Dexter background black
Qly, 1st and 4th, Gules a saltire engrailed or, on a chief or three cross
crosslets gules (Longe), 2nd and 3rd, Gules two leopards' faces in pale
between two flaunches or (Frere)   In pretence: Gules a chevron
ermine between three lions' gambs erased argent (Browne)   Also
impaling, Argent on a bend engrailed sable between two acorns proper
three fleurs-de-lys or (Ward)
Crest: A lion sejant gules holding a saltire engrailed or
Mantling: Gules and argent   Motto: In coelo quies   Skull in base
For the Rev. John Longe, who m. 1st, Charlotte, dau. and heir of John
Browne of Ipswich, and 2nd, Frances, dau. of Richard Ward, Esq., of

Salhouse Hall, Norfolk, and d.s.p. 3 Mar. 1834, aged 69.   (B.L.G.
7th ed.; E.A. N. and Q., VI, 35)

4. Sinister background black
Qly, 1st and 4th, Bacon, as 1, with crescent argent for difference,
2nd and 3rd, Barry of six or and azure over all a bend gules (Quaplode),
impaling, Browne, as 3.
Crest, mantling and motto: As 1.   Cherubs' heads at top corners of
shield
For Anna Maria, dau. of John Browne, of Ipswich, who m. 1780, the
Rev. Nicholas Bacon, and d. 9 Aug. 1783.   (E.A. N. and Q. (N.S.),
IV, 51)

5. All black background
Qly, as 4.   In pretence: Browne, as 3.
Crest: As 1, but with crescent sable for difference
Mantling and motto: As 1.
For the Rev. Nicholas Bacon, who m. Anna Maria, dau. of John
Browne, and d. 26 Aug. 1796, aged 65.   (Source, as 4.)

6. All black background
Qly, as 4, but no crescent for difference
Crest, mantling and motto: As 1.
Probably for a son of Nicholas Bacon and his wife, Dorothy Temple.
The following were buried at Coddenham: 1. Lionel, 21 Feb. 1735;
2. Philip, 1 Apr. 1738; 3. Montagu, 19 Apr. 1749.
(Coddenham Registers)

COWLINGE

1. Dexter background black
Paly of six argent and gules a lion passant proper, on a chief azure an
anchor or between two martlets argent, a molet argent on chief for
difference (Usborne), impaling, Azure three fleurs-de-lys or, on a chief
argent three molets sable   (Birch)
Crest: On a mount vert a hart lodged at the foot of a tree all proper
Mantling: Gules and argent   Motto: Resurgam
For Henry Usborne, of Branches Park, who m. Phoebe Ann, dau. of
Sir Joseph Birch, Bt., of the Hasles, Lancs, and d. 23 July 1840.
(B.P. 1868 ed.; Copinger, V, 208)

CROWFIELD

1. Identical to Barham No. 3
For Sir William Fowle Fowle Middleton, 2nd Bt., who m. 1825, Hon.

Anne Cust, dau. of Lord Brownlow, and d. 2 May 1860, aged 75.
(B.P. 1868 ed.; E.A. N. and Q., V, 341, VI, 36, 181)

DARSHAM

1. **Dexter background black**
Qly, 1st and 4th, Azure on a fess argent between three mascles or
three cinquefoils azure (Purvis), 2nd and 3rd, Sable a cross potent or
(Alleyn), impaling, Azure a chevron or gutty gules between three
molets of six points argent pierced azure (Cruttenden)
Crest: A sun in splendour rising from clouds proper, surmounted by a
scroll inscribed 'Clarior e tenebris'   Mantling: Gules and argent
Motto: Clarior e tenebris
For Charles Purvis, of Darsham House, who m. 1774, Elizabeth, dau. of
Edward Holden Cruttenden, and d. 10 Dec. 1808.   (Burke's
Commoners, Vol. 3; B.L.G. 1853 ed.)

2. **All black background**
Arms, as 1., but on a lozenge surmounted by a cherub's head
For Elizabeth, widow of Charles Purvis.   She d. 25 Mar. 1816.
(B.L.G. 1853 ed.)

DEBENHAM

1. **All black background**
Qly of eight, 1st and 8th, Vert a tortoise argent (Gawdy), 2nd, Argent
a fess between three Cornish choughs sable (Framlingham), 3rd, Gules a
goat salient argent armed or (Bardwell), 4th, Ermine on a chief sable
three crosses formy argent (Wichingham), 5th, Sable a pale lozengy
argent (Furneaux), 6th, Qly or and gules in the 1st quarter an eagle
displayed vert (Pakenham), 7th, Gyronny of twelve or and azure
(Bassingbourne)   In pretence: Or a chevron chequy gules and argent
between three cinquefoils azure (Cooke)
Crest: On a chapeau gules and ermine two swords palewise proper
Mantling: Gules and argent
For Sir Charles Gawdy, b. 1612, knighted 1639, who m. Vere, dau. and
co-heir of Sir Edward Cooke of Gidea Hall, Essex, and was buried at
Debenham, 24 Feb. 1650.   (B.E.B.; Millican's 'Gawdys of Norf. and
Suff., 45-8)

2. **Sinister background black**
Vert a tortoise argent on a canton argent the hand of Ulster (Gawdy),
impaling, Argent on a fess vert three lozenges or (Fielding)
Skull above shield

For Mary, dau. of George Fielding, Earl of Desmond, who m. 1657, as
his 1st wife, Charles Gawdy, cr. bt. 1661, and was buried at Debenham,
8 Sept. 1691.   (Sources, as 1)

DENSTON

1. All black background
Vert on a chevron between three stags trippant or three cinquefoils
gules (Robinson)
Crest: On a mount vert a stag trippant or   Mantling: Gules and argent
Motto: Resurgam
Possibly for John Nevill Robinson, Lieut. 43rd R.L.I., d. Dec. 1818,
aged 24; or his brother, William Henry Robinson, d. 23 Nov. 1826,
aged 42.   (Proc. S.I A., VI, 409-10)

2. Sinister background black
Robinson, impaling, Argent on a fess sable three molets or (Clive)
Motto: Celer atque fidelis   Two cherubs' heads above
For Rebecca, dau. of Robert, 1st Lord Clive, who m. 1780, Lt.-General
John Robinson, of Denston Hall, and d. 18 Nov. 1795, aged 34.
(B.P. 1891, under Powis;   Proc. S.I.A., VI, 407)

EASTON

1. All black background
Azure a chevron between three hanks of cotton argent (Cotton)
Crest: A falcon or holding in the dexter claw a belt sable buckled or
Mantling: Gules and argent
Probably for Dr. Ralph Cotton, M.D., of Yarmouth, b. 1642, d. unm.,
buried at Easton, 13 Aug. 1705.   (E.A. Miscellany, 1907, p. 3;
Brig. J. J. Packard)

2. Sinister background black
Qly of six, 1st, Argent on a bend gules cotised sable three pairs of wings
conjoined argent (Wingfield), 2nd, Qly or and sable (Bovill), 3rd, Or
three bars gules a canton ermine (Goushill), 4th, qly i. and iv. Gules a
lion rampant or (Arundel), ii. and iii. Chequy or and azure (Warren),
5th, Qly gules and or in the first quarter a molet argent (Vere), 6th,
Vert a lion rampant argent vulned on the shoulder gules (Bulbeke), in
fess point the Badge of Ulster, impaling, Qly, 1st and 4th, Argent a
chevron gules between three heraldic tigers' heads erased proper
(Jacob), 2nd and 3rd, Argent three boars passant each with a bone in
his mouth sable, a crescent gules for cadency (Abraham)
Cherub's head above   Gold leaves and buds on frame

For Susan, dau. of Sir John Jacob, Bt., of Bromley, Middlesex, who m.
1649, as his 1st wife, Sir Richard Wingfield, 2nd Bt., of Letheringham
and Easton, and d. 1652. (B.E.B.: Powerscourt's 'Wingfield
Memorials'; Proc. S.I.A., VII, 60)

3. **All black background**
Qly, 1st, Azure billetty a lion rampant or (Nassau), 2nd, Or a lion
rampant guardant gules ducally crowned azure (Dietz), 3rd, Gules a
fess argent (Vianden), 4th, Gules two lions passant guardant in pale
or (Catznellogen)   In pretence: Gules three millrinds argent a label
argent for difference (Zuleistein)
Crest: From a ducal coronet or a pair of bucks' horns gules
Mantling: Gules and argent   Motto: Spes durat avorum
Probably for Hon. Henry Nassau, son of 1st Earl of Rochford, d. unm.,
buried at Easton, 23 Apr. 1741.   (Brig. Packard)

4. Identical to 3., but with motto, In coelo quies
Winged skull in base
Unidentified

5. **Sinister background black**
Qly, 1st and 4th, qly i. and iv. Nassau, ii. Dietz, lion not guardant,
iii. Vianden, over all, Zuleistein, 2nd and 3rd, Argent six lions rampant
sable (Savage)
In pretence: Qly argent and gules a fret or over all on a bend sable
three escallops argent (Spencer)
Crest and motto: As 3.
On a lozenge to the sinister, Qly, 1st and 4th, qly i. and iv. Gules three
cinquefoils pierced ermine (Hamilton), ii. and iii. Argent a lymphad
with furled sails sable (Arran), 2nd and 3rd, Argent a human heart
gules imperially crowned proper, on a chief azure three molets argent
(Douglas)
In pretence: Spencer
The lozenge ensigned with a duchess's coronet, and below it the motto
'Through' A sinister supporter only to the lozenge; An antelope argent,
armed, ducally gorged, chained and hooved or (Hamilton)
For Anne, dau. and co-heir of Edward Spencer of Rendlesham, Suffolk,
and dowager of James, 5th Duke of Hamilton, who m. 2nd, 1751,
Richard Savage Nassau, 2nd son of Frederick, 3rd Earl of Rochford,
and d. 9 Mar. 1771.
(B.E.P.; B.P. 1953 ed.)

6. **All black background**
Qly, 1st, Nassau, 2nd, Dietz, 3rd, Vianden, tinctures reversed, 4th,
Catznellogen
Earl's coronet   Crest: As 3.   Mantle: Gules and ermine

Motto: As 3.   Supporters: Two lions guardant or ermined sable
ducally crowned azure
For William Henry Nassau, 5th Earl of Rochford, who d. unm. 1830.
(B.E.P.)

7. Dexter background black
Two shields   Dexter, within the Garter, Qly, 1st and 4th, qly i. and
iv. Hamilton, ii. and iii. Arran, 2nd and 3rd, qly i. Azure a lion rampant
argent crowned or (Galloway), ii. Or a lion rampant gules debruised by
a bendlet sable (Abernethy), iii. Argent three piles gules (Wishart),
iv. Or a fess chequy azure and argent over all a bend gules charged with
three buckles or (Stewart); over the 2nd and 3rd qrs an escutcheon,
Argent a human heart gules imperially crowned proper, on a chief azure
three molets argent (Douglas); and over all a crowned escutcheon of
France for Chatelherault
Sinister shield, as dexter, impaling, Qly, 1st and 4th, Per pale gules
and azure on a chevron argent between three martlets or an eagle displayed sable, all within a bordure or charged with a double tressure
flory-counter-flory gules (Beckford), 2nd and 3rd, qly i. and iv. Hamilton, ii. and iii. Arran
Duke's coronet above dexter shield.   Crests: Dexter, from a ducal
coronet or a frame saw or cutting an oak tree proper, on a scroll the
motto 'Through'   Sinister, on a chapeau gules and ermine a salaman-
der in flames proper, on a scroll the motto 'Jamais arriere' (Douglas)
Motto: (below) Through
Supporters: Two antelopes argent, attired, ducally gorged and chained
or
For Alexander, 10th Duke of Hamilton, who m. 1810, Susan
Euphemia, dau. and co-heir of William Beckford, of Fonthill Abbey,
and d. 18 Aug. 1852.
(B.P. 1953 ed.)

8. All black background
A shield and a lozenge   Dexter (shield), as dexter shield of 7. within
the Garter   Sinister (lozenge), as sinister shield of 7.
Duchess's coronet   Supporters: As 7.
For Susan Euphemia, widow of Alexander, 10th Duke of Hamilton.
She d. 27 May 1859.   (B.P. 1953 ed.)

9. Dexter background black
Qly, 1st and 4th, qly i. and iv. Hamilton, ii. and iii. Arran, 2nd and 3rd,
qly, i. Galloway, ii. Abernethy, iii. Wishart, iv. Stewart; over the 1st and
4th qrs a crowned escutcheon of France, for Chatelherault, and over
the 2nd and 3rd qrs an escutcheon of Douglas
In pretence: Or a bend gules, ensigned with a royal coronet (Princess
Mary of Baden)
Duke's coronet   Crests, and crest mottoes: As 7.
Supporters: Dexter, An antelope argent attired, ducally gorged and
chained or (Hamilton)   Sinister, A griffin reguardant, wings expanded
and royally crowned or (Baden)

For William, 11th Duke of Hamilton, who m. 1843, Princess Mary of
Baden, and d. 15 July 1863. (B.P. 1953 ed.)

ELMSETT

1. **All black background**
Qly, 1st and 4th, Sable three griffins' heads erased argent (Skinner),
2nd and 3rd, Sable a cross between four pheons or (Jones)
Crest: A griffin's head erased argent   Mantling: Gules and argent
Motto: Coelitas mihi vires (Jones, Viscount Ranelagh)   Skull in base
Unidentified

EYE

1. **All black background**
On a lozenge   Or on a chief indented azure two molets or (D'Eye),
impaling, Gules a bend engrailed between six lions rampant or (Cowper)
Crest: Two wings expanded or   Mantling: Gules and argent
For Mary (née Cowper) who m. Nathaniel D'Eye, and d. 27 Dec. 1749,
aged 85.   He d. 29 Jan. 1718, aged 68.
(Cullum's 'Cullum Family', 46-7; Proc. S.I.A., II, 147)

2. **Dexter background black**
Gules a chevron ermine between three seagulls argent (Sayer), impaling,
Argent two chevrons azure within a bordure engrailed gules (Tyrell)
Crest: A hand proper holding a dragon's head erased argent
Mantling: Gules and argent   Motto: In coelo quies   Skull in base
For John Sayer, who m. Grace, dau. of Thomas Tyrell, of Gipping Hall,
and d. 3 Jan. 1761, aged 89.   She d. 13 Nov. 1775, aged 61.
(Proc. S.I.A., II, 144)

3. **All black background**
Argent a pall between two castles sable (Cunningham), impaling, two
coats per fess, in chief, Argent a fess sable in chief three grenades sable
inflamed proper (Wymond), in base, Ermine on a fess gules a lion
passant or (Proby)
Crest: A unicorn's head couped argent, armed and maned or
Mantling: Gules and argent   Motto: Vince malum bono
Stars of two Orders suspended below shield
For Rear-Admiral Sir Charles Cunningham, K.G.H., who d. 11 Feb.
1834, aged 78.   (Proc. S.I.A., II, 145)

FORNHAM ALL SAINTS

1. **All black background**
On a lozenge   Sable three esquires' helms argent (Halliday), impaling, Qly, 1st and 4th, Sable a chevron between three pickaxes argent (Moseley), 2nd, Argent a fess wavy between three leopards' faces gules (Goodday), 3rd, Gules three leopards' faces or ( )
For Sarah Elizabeth, elder dau. of William Moseley, of Fornham All Saints, who m. Robert Halliday, of Somerset, and d. 7 Apr. 1834.
(B.L.G. 1853 ed; Gage's 'Thingoe Hundred', 244)

FORNHAM ST. MARTIN

1. **All black background**
Argent a chevron engrailed vert between in chief two escutcheons gules each charged with a caltrap argent and in base a talbot's head erased proper, in centre chief the Badge of Ulster (Gilstrap), impaling, Azure a saltire engrailed ermine, in chief and in base a rock proper, in dexter fess a decrescent, in sinister fess an increscent argent; on the saltire an estoile azure (Haigh)
Crest: Upon a rock a forearm erect, mailed proper, the hand holding an escutcheon gules charged with a caltrap argent
Mantling: Vert and argent   Motto: Candide secure
For Sir William Gilstrap, Bt., of Fornham Park, who m. 1847, Elizabeth, dau. of Thomas Haigh, of co. Yorks, and d. 15 Feb. 1896.
(B.P. 1891 ed.; Copinger, VI, 270)

2. **All black background**
Within the Garter, Qly, 1st, Gules on a bend between six cross crosslets fitchy argent the Augmentation of Flodden (Howard), 2nd, Gules three lions passant guardant in pale or a label of three points argent (Brotherton), 3rd, Chequy or and azure (Warren), 4th, Gules a lion rampant argent (Mowbray)
Behind the shield two batons in saltire, the insignia of the Earl Marshal
Duke's coronet   Crests: 1. From a ducal coronet or a pair of wings gules each charged with a bend between six cross crosslets fitchy argent
2. On a chapeau gules and ermine a lion statant guardant with tail extended or, gorged with a ducal coronet argent   3. On a mount vert a horse passant argent holding in the mouth a slip of oak fructed proper
Mantle: Gules and ermine   Motto: Sola virtus invicta
Supporters: Dexter, A lion argent   Sinister, A horse argent holding in the mouth a slip of oak fructed proper
For Bernard, 12th Duke of Norfolk, m. 1789, Lady Elizabeth Belasyse, divorced 1794. He d. 16 Mar. 1842.   (B.P. 1891 ed.; Copinger, VI, 269)

3. All black background
On a lozenge   Or two bars azure a crescent azure charged with
another argent for difference (Manners), impaling, Qly of six, 1st,
Argent a cross calvary gules (Butler), 2nd, Or a chief indented azure a
crescent gules (Butler), 3rd, Gules three covered cups or a crescent
argent (Butler), 4th, Ermine a saltire gules (Fitzgerald), 5th, Per pale
indented or and gules (? Bermingham), 6th, Argent an eagle displayed
sable between four crosses formy gules (   )
Baroness's coronet   Supporters: Two unicorns argent armed and
unguled or, the dexter charged with a cross flory and the sinister with
a portcullis sable
For Jane, dau. of James, 9th Lord Caher, who m. 1815, as his second
wife, Thomas, 1st Lord Manners, and d. 2 Nov. 1846.   (B.P. 1949
ed.)
(This hatchment was badly damaged when recorded by Mr. Harold
Hawes in 1952, and for this reason may well have been incorrectly
blazoned. It was destroyed before 1962.)

FRAMLINGHAM

1. All black background
On a lozenge   Sable on a pile argent a caltrap sable (Kerridge)
In pretence: Sable three bells argent a chief ermine (Porter)
Cherub's head above
For Jane, dau. and heir of Richard Porter of Framlingham, who m.
Thomas Kerridge of Shelley Hall, and d. 5 Sept. 1744.   (Green's
'Framlingham and Saxted', 148-9)
(Husband's hatchment is in Shelley church.)

2. All black background
Azure a chevron between three talbots' heads erased argent collared
gules a label of three points argent for cadency (Alexander)
Crest: A talbot's head erased argent collared gules
Mantling: Gules and argent   Motto: Christus vita morte
Skulls at each corner of frame, crossbones on sides
Possibly for Joseph Alexander, d. 26 Sept. 1644, aged 24, or John
Alexander, d. 10 Apr. 1661, aged 42.   (Green, 140-1)

GIPPING

1. All black background
Qly, 1st and 4th, Argent two chevronels azure a bordure engrailed gules
(Tyrell), 2nd and 3rd, Sable a fess argent between three escallops or
(Bright)

Crest: A boar's head erect couped argent, issuant from the mouth a
peacock's tail proper   Mantling: Gules and argent
Motto: Resurgam
Supporters: Two panthers proper   Cherub's head in base
For Edmund Tyrell, of Gipping Hall, son of Edmund Tyrell and his
second wife, Mary Bright.   Born 1744, d. unm. 30 Mar. 1799.
(Bright's 'Brights of Suffolk', 229)

HACHESTON

1. Dexter background black
Qly, 1st and 4th, Argent three chevronels sable (Arcedeckne), 2nd and
3rd, Argent on a chief embattled sable three bezants (Leigh), impaling,
Qly, 1st and 4th, Per pale gules and azure on a chevron between three
martlets argent three eagles displayed sable (Beckford), 2nd, Argent
three bars and in chief three lions' heads erased gules (Love), 3rd,
Argent on a chief embattled sable three bezants (Leigh)
Crest: An arm embowed mailed proper in the hand a sword, pommel
and hilt or   Mantling: Gules and argent   Motto: Deus providebit
For Andrew Arcedeckne of Glevering Hall, who m. 1816, Harriet, only
dau. of Francis Love Beckford, and d. 1849.   (B.L.G. 1853 ed.)

HADLEIGH

1. Dexter background black
Argent on a bend sable three chessrooks argent in chief a crescent sable
for difference (Bunbury)   In pretence: Ermine a lion rampant
azure (Eyton)
No crest or mantling   Motto: Hora pars vitae
For William, 2nd son of Sir Henry Bunbury, 2nd Bt.   He m. Sarah,
dau. and co-heir of Sir James Eyton and d. 1748.   (Darby MS.,
Ips. Ref. Lib.; Betham's 'Baronetage' III, 50)

2. Dexter background black
Qly, 1st and 4th, Azure three molets argent (   ), 2nd and 3rd,
Argent a crescent sable (Wilkins), impaling, Argent three bars gemel
gules, over all a lion rampant sable (Fairfax)
Motto: Non est mortuis quod optus
For the Rev. David Wilkins, D.D., Rector of Hadleigh, who m. 1725,
Margaret, dau. of Thomas, Lord Fairfax, and d. 6 Sept. 1745, aged 60.
(Proc. S.I.A., III, 205-11)

3. Dexter background black
Qly, 1st, Or a unicorn rampant azure within a bordure gules charged
with ten roundels argent (Drummond), 2nd, Argent three escutcheons

gules (Hay), 3rd, Argent three bars wavy gules, over all a scimitar bend-
ways proper (Drummond), 4th, Or a lion's head erased within a double
tressure flory-counter-flory gules (Strathalan), impaling two coats per
fess, in chief, Azure a chevron between in chief two molets and in base
a crescent or (Visme), and in base, Argent on a mount vert a tree, on
top thereof a bird; pendent from the tree, one on either side of the
trunk a bird's nest, all proper (Auriol)
Crest: A demi-man vested grey, capped azure, waistcoat gules, bearing
on his shoulder an ox-yoke proper
Motto: (above) Renovate animos, (below) Spes mea in Deo
For the Very Rev. Edward Auriol Hay-Drummond, who m. 1st, 1782,
Elizabeth, dau. of William de Visme, and 2nd, Amelia, dau. of James
Auriol, and d. 30 Dec. 1829.   (B.P. 1939 ed.; Proc. S.I.A., III,
282-3)

4. Sinister background black
Argent three blackamoors' heads couped proper wreathed at the
temples argent and gules, drops in their ears argent (Tanner), impaling,
Sable a fess ermine between three cinquefoils argent (Potter)
Crest: A blackamoor's head as in the arms   Mantling: Gules and
argent
Motto: In coelo quies   Cherubs' heads at top corner and base of
shield
For Mary, dau. of Archbishop Potter, who m. Thomas Tanner, D.D.,
Rector of Hadleigh, and d. 30 Apr. 1779, aged 56.   He d. 11 Mar.
1786, aged 68.
(Proc. S.I.A., III, 281)

HALESWORTH

1. All black background
Qly of six, 1st, Barry nebuly of six argent and sable a canton gules
(Keble), 2nd, Lozengy argent and sable (Croftes), 3rd, Argent two
chevronels gules within a bordure sable (Pannell), 4th, Argent on a
chevron engrailed sable three escallops argent (King), 5th, Gules three
chevronels argent (Fettiplace), 6th, Gules a griffin segreant argent
(Went)
Crest: A griffin's head erased or   Mantling: Gules and argent
Motto: Nec flatu nec fluctu
Frame decorated with carved cherubs' heads and leaves
Probably for John Keble, of Halesworth, d. unm. 1652 or 1653.
(Suckling, II, 279)

HARTEST

1. All black background

Qly, 1st and 4th, Or on a pile engrailed sable three cross crosslets or, in base two fountains (Hallifax), 2nd and 3rd, Argent on a bend sable three owls argent (Savile), impaling, Qly, 1st and 4th, Argent two chevronels within a bordure engrailed sable (Staunton), 2nd and 3rd, Or three bends gules (   )

Crests: Dexter, A moorcock displayed per bend sinister sable and gules ducally gorged or, on its breast a cross crosslet or   Sinister: An owl proper (Savile)   Mantling: Gules and argent

Motto: Sacre cheveux

For Thomas Hallifax, of Chadacre Hall, in Shimpling, who m. Anna Maria, dau. of John Staunton of Kenilworth, and d. 1850.

(B.L.G. 1853 ed.)

HAUGHLEY

1. All black background

Azure on a chief indented or three martlets gules (Ray)   In pretence: Argent a lion rampant double-queued sable gorged with a collar flory-counter-flory or (Walklate)

Crest: An ostrich or in its beak a horseshoe azure

Motto: Resurgemus

For Rev. Richard Ray, Vicar of Haughley for 55 years, m. 1701, Margaret Walklate, of Uttoxeter, Staffs, and d. 8 May 1758, aged 83. She d. 1753, aged 72.   (Cullum's 'Ray of Denston', 18)

2. Dexter background black

Qly, 1st and 4th, Azure on a chief indented or three martlets gules (Ray), 2nd and 3rd, Argent a lion rampant double-queued sable gorged with a collar flory-counter-flory or (Walklate)   In pretence: Qly, 1st and 4th, Per fess azure and or a pale and three falcons, wings addorsed and belled, each holding in the beak a padlock, all counter changed (Lock), 2nd, Or a cross formy gules between four eagles displayed sable (Dixon), 3rd, Chequy or and sable a fess ermine (Buckham)

Crest: An ostrich or in its beak a horseshoe azure

Mantling: Gules and argent   Motto: Et juste et vray

For Richard Ray, of Plashwood in Haughley, b. 1721, m. 1770, Elizabeth, heir of John Lock of Mildenhall, and d. 16 Feb. 1811. ('Ray of Denston', 19)

3. Dexter background black

Gules on a bend between six unicorns' heads erased argent a crescent gules for difference, in chief the Badge of Ulster (Wombwell), impaling,

Gules two bars gemel between three escallops argent (Rawlinson)
Crest: A unicorn's head erased argent   Mantling: Gules and argent
Motto: In coelo quies   Cherubs' heads at top corners of shield
Skull in base
For Sir George Wombwell, 1st Bt., who m. 1765, Susanna, only dau. of
Sir Thomas Rawlinson, and d. 2 Nov. 1780.   (B.P. 1939 ed.: 'Ray of
Denston', 18-19)

4. **All black background**
Per fess indented azure and argent (Crawford), impaling, Argent a lion
rampant within a bordure engrailed sable semy of molets argent
(Cowley)
Crest: A stag's head couped proper
Mantling: Gules and argent   Motto: Conquiesco
For William Crawford, of Haughley Park, who m. Elizabeth Dorothie
Cowley, and d. 5 Nov. 1835, aged 79.   (Copinger, VI, 205)
(Hatchment of wife, *see* Wetherden I.)

5. **Sinister background black**
Argent two chevronels azure within a bordure engrailed gules (Tyrell)
In pretence: Azure on a chief indented or three martlets gules (Ray)
Crest: A boar's head couped and erect argent, out of the mouth a
peacock's tail proper   Mantling: Gules and argent   Motto:
Resurgam
Supporters: Two panthers proper
For Elizabeth, dau. and heir of Richard Ray, who m. 1801, Charles
Tyrell, of Gipping Hall, and d. 22 Aug. 1826.   He d. 2 Jan. 1872.
('Ray of Denston', 19-20)

HAVERHILL

1. **All black background**
Argent two bars and in chief three lions rampant sable (Howland)
Crest: An ounce passant sable ducally gorged or
Mantling: Gules and argent   Motto: In coelo quies
Probably for George Howland, lord of the manor of Haverhill from
1768 to at least 1784.   (MS. Court book)

HAWKEDON

1. **Dexter background black**
Ermine on a chief gules three lions rampant argent (Oliver)
In pretence: Or on a chief sable three lions' heads erased or
(Richardson)
Crest: A lion's gamb erased holding an olive branch fructed, all proper

Mantling: Gules and argent

For John Oliver, who m. Harriet, dau of Thomas Richardson, of Long
Melford, widow of Philip Hamond (*see* 3.), and d.   (Copinger, V,
245)
(Hatchment of wife, *see* Long Melford 5.)

2. Dexter background black
Ermine a bend vairy or and gules cotised gules (Plume), impaling, Per
pale gules and azure three demi-lions passant guardant or (Hamond)
Crest: A talbot sejant gules collared or   Mantling: Gules and argent
On sinister side of frame, skulls and crossbones; on dexter side, ? ferns
For Edmund Plume of Hawkedon Hall, who m. Anne, sister of Philip
Hamond, and d. 29 Jan. 1708.   She d. 28 Aug. 1722, aged 91.
(Mills MS.; Copinger, V, 245)

3. All black background
Or on a chief sable three lions' heads erased or (Richardson), impaling,
Per pale gules and azure three demi-lions passant guardant or (Hamond)
Crest: A talbot sejant gules collared or (Plume)
Mantling: Gules and argent   Motto: In coelo quies
For Philip Hamond, of Hawkedon Hall, who m. Harriet Richardson
(*see* 1.), and d. 18 July 1779, aged 30.   (Mills MS.; Copinger, V,
245)
(N.B.—A very inaccurate hatchment. The impaled coats are reversed
and the crest is for Plume)

HAWSTEAD

1. All black background
On a lozenge   Argent three calves passant sable (Metcalfe)
Motto: Resurgam
Probably for Lucy, dau. of Christopher Metcalfe and his wife, Ellen
Barton.   She d. 1793, aged 24.   (Cullum's 'Hawstead'; Gage's
Thingoe')

2. Sinister background black
Qly, 1st and 4th, Azure a lion rampant or a label of three points argent
(Colvile), 2nd and 3rd, Azure a tower or (   ), impaling, Argent
three calves passant sable (Metcalfe)
Mantling: Gules and argent   Motto: Resurgam   Cherub's head
above
For Emma, dau. of Christopher Barton Metcalfe, who m. 1825, as his
first wife, the Rev. Nathaniel Colvile, and d. 14 Feb. 1840.
(B.L.G. 1853 ed.; Mon. Hawstead church; Colvile's 'History of Colvile
Family', 66)

3. All black background
Argent on a chevron sable between three roundels sable each charged
with a martlet argent three escallops or, all within a bordure engrailed
vert (Hammond), impaling, Gules a bend ermine between two hawks
close or (Asty)
Crest: Out of a ducal coronet or a demi-eagle wings displayed or
Mantling: Gules and argent   Motto: Mors janua vitae   Skull in
base
For Francis Hammond, of London and Hawstead, who m. Honor. dau.
of Ambrose Asty, of Herts, and d. 1727/8.   (Gage's 'Thingoe', 395;
Muskett's 'Suffolk Manorial Families', I, 264)

4. Sinister background black
Argent three calves passant sable (Metcalfe), impaling, Azure a chevron
between three lions' heads erased or, on a chief argent a rose gules
between two griffins' heads sable (? Whish)
Motto: Resurgam
? For Frances Jane, dau. of Martin Whish, who m. Henry Metcalfe, of
Hawstead House, and d. 29 Apr. 1830, aged 37; buried at Hawstead,
10 May.   (Par. Reg.)

5. All black background
Metcalfe   To dexter of main shield, Metcalfe, impaling, ? Whish
S.Bl.   To sinister of main shield, Metcalfe, impaling, Argent a forearm
in armour or the hand holding a battleaxe sable (   )   D.Bl.
Crest: A talbot sejant sable supporting an escutcheon or
Mantling: Gules and argent   Motto: Resurgam
? For Henry Metcalfe, of Hawstead House, who m. (? 1st), Frances
Jane, dau. of Martin Whish.   He was buried at Hawstead, 8 Sept.
1849, aged 58.
(Par. Reg.)

HEMINGSTONE

1. All black background
On a lozenge   Argent two bars gules (Martin)
Motto: In coelo quies
For a dau. of William Martin and his wife, Sarah Rowley (*see* 4)
Philadelphia, d. 14 Aug. 1842, aged 45; Arabella Mary, d. 10 Mar.
1855, aged 64; Maria, d. 20 Mar. 1870, aged 71.   (E.A. N. and Q.,
V, 355-6)

2. Dexter background black
Martin, impaling, Argent a fess between three boars' heads couped
close sable (Verner)
Crest: A monkey proper collared or admiring himself in a mirror
proper

Mantling: Gules and argent   Motto: Sans tache
For Richard Bartholomew Martin, of Hemingstone Hall, who m. 1832,
Juliana, dau. of John Donovan Verner, of Dublin, and d. 11 Apr. 1865,
aged 53.
(B.L.G. 1900 ed.; E.A. N. and Q., V, 355-6)

3. Sinister background black
On a lozenge surmounted by a cherub's head
Martin, impaling, Argent on a bend sable between two choughs proper
three escallops argent (Rowley)
Mantling: Gules and argent
For Sarah, dau. of Admiral Sir Joshua Rowley, Bt., who m. 1787, her
cousin, William Martin, of Hemingstone Hall, and d. 21 Dec. 1841.
(Mon. in church; B.L.G. 1853 ed.; E.A. N. and Q, V, 355-6)

4. All black background
Arms, as 3., but bend engrailed
Crest: A fox proper (should be an ape) collared and lined or, admiring
himself in a mirror proper   Mantling: Gules and argent
Motto: Resurgam
For William Martin, of Hemingstone Hall, who m. Sarah, dau. of
Admiral Sir Joshua Rowley, Bt., and d. 13 Nov. 1842, aged 81.
(Sources, as 3.)

HENGRAVE

1. All black background
Qly, 1st and 4th, Per saltire azure and argent a saltire gules (Gage), 2nd,
Argent three cinquefoils gules (D'Arcy), 3rd, Or three quatrefoils
gules (D'Ewes), over all the Badge of Ulster
Crest: A ram passant argent armed and unguled or
Mantling: Gules and argent   Motto: Bon temps viendra
For Sir Thomas Gage, 3rd Bt., d. unm. 1 Sept. 1741.   (B.P. 1868
ed.; Gage's 'Hengrave' and 'Thingoe'; Copinger, VII, 56-60)

2. Dexter background black
Qly, 1st and 4th, Per saltire azure and argent (Gage), 2nd and 3rd,
Argent six chessrooks, three, two, one sable (Rookwood), impaling,
Argent a lion rampant gules, on a chief azure a cross crosslet between a
molet and a rose argent, a molet gules for difference (Fergus), the
Badge of Ulster over line of impalement
Crest, mantling and motto: As 1.
For Sir Thomas Rookwood Gage, 5th Bt., who m. 1st, 1746, Lucy,
dau. of William Knight, of co. Lincs, and 2nd, 1783, Mary, dau. of
Patrick Fergus of the Island of Montserrat.   He d. 21 Mar. 1796,
aged 77.   (Sources, as 1)

3. **Sinister background black**
Qly, 1st and 4th, Gage, as 2., 2nd, Rookwood with label for difference,
3rd, Argent three bendlets gules on a canton azure a spur or (Knight),
impaling, Gules three lions rampant or (Fitzherbert)
Mantling: Gules and argent   Cherub's head above shield and skull
below
For Charlotte, dau. of Thomas Fitzherbert, of Swinnerton, Staffs, and
1st wife of Sir Thomas Gage, 6th Bt.   She m. 1779, and d. 29 Aug.
1790, aged 34.   (Sources, as 1.)

4. **Dexter background black**
Qly, 1st, Gage, as 1., with crescent for difference and Badge of Ulster,
2nd, Azure a sun in splendour proper (St. Clere), 3rd, Rookwood,
4th, Knight, impaling, Qly, 1st, Or a stag's head cabossed sable attired
gules (Calder), 2nd, Gyronny of eight or and sable (Campbell), 3rd,
Argent a galley sable (Lorne), 4th, Per fess azure and gules a cross or
(   )
Crest, mantling and motto: As 1.   Winged skull below shield
For Sir Thomas Gage, 6th Bt., who m. 1st, 1779, Charlotte, dau. of
Thomas Fitzherbert, and 2nd, 1796, Charlotte, dau. of John Hook
Campbell, of Bangerston, co. Pembroke, and d. 1 Dec. 1798, aged 47.
(Sources, as 1.)

5. **Dexter background black**
Qly, 1st and 4th, Gage, as 1., 2nd and 3rd, Rookwood, over all the
Badge of Ulster, impaling, Qly, 1st and 4th, Or three bars wavy gules
(Drummond), 2nd and 3rd, Or a lion's head erased within a double
tressure flory-counter-flory gules (Drummond)
Crest, mantling and motto: As 1.
For Sir Thomas Rookwood-Gage, 8th Bt., who m. 1850, Adelaide, dau.
and co-heir of Henry Drummond, of Albury Park, Surrey, and d. 7 June
1866.   (Sources, as 1.; Howard's 'Visit. of Suff.', II, 108)

6. **Dexter background black**
Qly, 1st and 4th, Gage, as 1., 2nd and 3rd, Rookwood, over all the
Badge of Ulster, impaling, Qly, 1st and 4th, qly i. and iv. France and
England quarterly, ii. Scotland, iii. Ireland; over all a baton sinister
gules charged with three roses argent (Beauclerk), 2nd and 3rd, Qly
gules and or in the first quarter a molet argent (Vere)
Crests: Dexter, A ram passant argent armed or (motto above in-
decipherable) Sinister, A chessrook sable between two wings argent
Mantling: Gules and argent
For Sir Edward Rookwood-Gage, 9th Bt., who m. 1842, Henrietta
Mary, dau. of the Rev. Lord Frederick Beauclerk, and d.s.p. 3 Jan.
1872.   (Sources, as 5.)

HENLEY

1. All black background
On a lozenge   Gules on a bend cotised argent between two fleeces
or three escallops gules (Ibbetson)
Mantling: Gules and argent   Motto: Vixi liber et moriar
For Harriet Ibbetson, 3rd dau. of Sir James Ibbetson, 2nd Bt. of
Denton Park, Yorks.   She d. 30 Oct. 1843, aged 67.   (B.P. 1891
ed.; E.A. N. and Q, VI, 12)

2. All black background
On a lozenge surmounted by a helm
Qly, 1st, Or on a chevron between three roses azure three pineapples
or (Gould), 2nd, Argent two bars gules a bordure sable (Gelsthorp),
3rd, Argent five cross crosslets gules (Cross), 4th, Sable a chevron
between three bulls' heads cabossed argent (Bulkeley), impaling, Argent
a chevron between three lozenges sable ermined argent (Shaw)
Mantling: Gules and argent   Motto: Mors janua vitae
For Henrietta, dau. of John Gould of Grundisburgh Hall and his wife
Henrietta Shaw, who m. 1767, Thomas Sleorgin, Cornet in the Horse
Guards, and d. 28 Apr. 1808.   (E.A. N. and Q, VI, 12, 71-2)
(Husband evidently non-armigerous, the arms being those of her
parents)

3. Sinister background black
Qly, 1st, Sable a fess embattled between three owls argent (Theobald),
2nd, Azure a chevron ermine between three pelicans vulning or
(Medows), 3rd, Gules on a chief argent a lion passant guardant gules
(Brooke), 4th, Sable a chevron argent between three boys' heads
couped at the shoulders having snakes about their necks proper
(Vaughan)
Crest: On a chapeau gules and ermine a cock gules   Mantling: Gules
and argent   Motto: In coelo quies
For Mary, dau. of William Snell of Needham Market, who m. as his first
wife, John Medows Theobald of Claydon Hall, and d. 27 Nov. 1809,
aged 56.   E.A. N. and Q, VI, 12, 71; do. (N.S.) IV, 158)
(Arms of husband only; wife evidently non-armigerous)

HENSTEAD

1. All black background
Argent on a cross between four frets gules a tower or (Bence)
Crest: A tower or charged with a fret gules
Mantling: Gules and argent
A very small hatchment

For Lawrence Bence, d. unm., buried at Henstead, 2 Apr. 1746, aged 41.
(Hill's 'Registers of Thorington'; B.L.G. 1853 ed.)

2. **All black background**
Azure on a fess engrailed between three griffins' heads erased or a fleur-de-lys vert between two roses gules (Sheriffe), impaling, Gules a saltire or between four fleurs-de-lys argent (Farr)
Crest: A lion's paw erased or holding a branch of dates stalked and leaved vert pods argent fruit or   Mantling: Gules and argent
Motto: Esse quam videri
For the Rev. Thomas Sheriffe, of Henstead Hall, Rector of Henstead, who m. 1823, Georgiana, dau. of Thomas Farr, of Beccles and North Cove, and d. 10 Oct. 1861, aged 70.   (Crisp's 'Visitation of England and Wales', X, 140)

HERRINGFLEET

1. **Dexter background black**
Azure on a bend between three fleurs-de-lys or three pierced molets gules (Leathes), impaling, Sable a swan wings addorsed argent within a bordure engrailed or (Moore)
Crest: A demi-griffin or armed gules   Mantling: Gules and argent
Motto: Resurgam
For George Leathes, of Herringfleet Hall, who m. Mary, dau. of J. Moore of co. Worcs, and d. 1817.   (B.L.G. 1853 ed.; Suckling, II, 14)

2. **All black background**
On a lozenge surmounted by an escallop
Arms: As 1.
Mantling and motto: As 1.
For Mary, widow of George Leathes.   She d.   (Sources, as 1.)

3. **Sinister background black**
Gules of a fess engrailed between three water bougets argent three cloves sable (Merry)   In pretence: Sable a griffin passant or between three crescents argent (Death)
Mantling: Gules and argent   Motto: In coelo quies
Skull and crossbones in base
For Elizabeth Death, widow of John Leathes (d.s.p. 1788, elder brother of George, see 1.), who m. Anthony Merry, and d. 4 Mar. 1824.
(B.L.G. 1853 ed.; Suckling, II, 14; Darby MS., Ips., Ref. Lib.)

HINTLESHAM

1. **Sinister background black**
On a lozenge   Sable three escutcheons argent each with a bordure
engrailed or (Burrell), impaling, Qly, 1st and 4th, Argent a heraldic
tiger statant reguardant sable (Daniell), 2nd and 3rd, Argent a pale
fusilly sable (Daniell)
Mantling: Gules and argent   Motto: Animus non officit oequus
Cherub's head above
For Frances, dau. of James Daniell, who m. 1807, the Hon. Lindsey
Merrik Peter Burrell, and d. 25 Aug. 1846, aged 67.   (B.P. 1891 ed.:
E.A. Misc. 1932, 21; E.A. N. and Q., XIII, 86)

2. **All black background**
Sable three horses' heads erased argent (Lloyd)
Crest: A horse's head erased argent   Mantling: Gules and argent
Motto: In coelo quies
For Capt. Heneage Lloyd, Coldstream Guards, d. unm. 22 Dec. 1776,
aged 33.
(Mills MS.; E.A. Misc. 1932, 65-6, 79, 81; E.A. N. and Q., XIII, 86)

HOLBROOK

1. **Dexter background black**
Qly, 1st and 4th, Argent a saltire vairy or and azure between four
Cornish choughs proper (Reade), 2nd and 3rd, Or ermined sable on a
chevron embattled gules three estoiles or, all within a bordure engrailed
sable (Revell), impaling, Argent a chevron azure between three garbs
proper (   )
Crest: On a mount vert a chough standing among reeds proper
Mantling: Gules and argent   Motto: Cedant arma togae
For John Reade of Holbrook House, who d. 7 July 1843, aged 72.
(E.A. N. and Q., VIII, 118)

HUNSTON

1. **Sinister background black**
Qly, 1st, Sable a fess chequy or and azure between three horses' heads
erased argent (Heigham), 2nd, Gules a chevron engrailed ermine
between three falcons rising argent (Francis), 3rd, Sable a chevron
engrailed between three fleurs-de-lys or, on a chief or three spearheads
azure (Wright), 4th, Ermine on a canton azure a pelican vulning herself
or (Pell), impaling, Qly, 1st and 4th, Sable a dolphin embowed swallow-
ing a fish or (Symonds), 2nd, Argent a chevron between three mascles

gules (Spring), 3rd, Sable a crescent between two molets in pale argent
(Jermyn)
Mantling: Gules and argent   Motto: Resurgam
For Elizabeth, dau. of Capt. Thomas Symonds, R.N., of Bury, who m.
1790, the Rev. Henry Heigham, of Hunston Hall, and d. 9 Dec. 1832.
(B.L.G. 1900 ed.; Tablet in church)

2. All black background
Arms: As 1.
Crest: A horse's head erased argent   Mantling: Azure and argent
Motto: Resurgam
For the Rev. Henry Heigham, d. 29 Dec. 1834.   (B.L.G. 1900 ed.;
Tablet in church)

3. Sinister background black
Qly, as dexter of 1., impaling, Per saltire or and azure a lion rampant
counterchanged (Gould)
Mantling: Gules and argent   Motto: Resurgam   Escallop in base
For Maria Catherine, dau. of Lt.-Col. William Gould of Bury, who m.
1823, as his first wife, John Henry Heigham, and d. 29 Nov. 1837,
aged 40.
(B.L.G. 1900 ed.; Tablet in church; 'Ray of Denston', 38)

HUNTINGFIELD

1. All black background
Argent a roundel between three hunting horns stringed gules in chief
the Badge of Ulster (Vanneck), impaling, Azure a chevron between
three acorns pendent or (Daubuz)
Crest: A hunting horn gules between two wings per fess or and argent
Mantle: Gules and argent with gold cords and tassels
Motto: Memoria pii aeterna   Cherubs' heads at sides of shield and
winged skull in base
For Sir Joshua Vanneck, 1st Bt., who m. 1732, Mary Anne, dau. of
Stephen Daubuz, and d. 5 Mar. 1777, aged 77.   (B.P. 1891 ed.;
Suckling, II, 419)

2. All black background
Vanneck, with Badge of Ulster
Crest, mantle and motto: As 1.   Cherub's heads and skull: As 1.
For Sir Gerard Vanneck, 2nd Bt., who d. unm. 23 May 1791, aged 48.
(Sources, as 1.)

3. Sinister background black
Vanneck, with Badge of Ulster in centre chief, impaling, Argent a stag's

head cabossed gules on a chief or a cross crosslet fitchy between two
molets gules (Thompson)
Baroness's coronet   Mantle: Gules and ermine   Supporters: Two
greyhounds ermine collared paly of six or and gules chained or
For Maria, dau. of Andrew Thompson, of Roehampton, who m. 1777,
Joshua, 1st Baron Huntingfield, and d. 7 Dec. 1811.   (B.P. 1891 ed.)

4. All black background
Vanneck, with Badge of Ulster, impaling, Thompson
Baron's coronet   Crest: As 1.
Mantle: Gules and ermine   Motto: Droit et loyal
Supporters: As 3.
For Joshua, 1st Baron Huntingfield, who d. 15 Aug. 1816.
(B.P. 1891 ed.; Suckling, II, 420)

5. Dexter background black
Vanneck, with Badge of Ulster, impaling, to the dexter, Argent three
chevronels sable, on the centre one three bezants (Arcedeckne), and to
the sinister,Gules a bend vair between two fleurs-de-lys argent (Blois)
Baron's coronet   Crest: (hidden by torn canvas)
Motto: As 4.   Supporters: As 3.
For Joshua, 2nd Baron Huntingfield, who m. 1st, 1810, Catherine, dau.
of Chaloner Arcedeckne, of Glevering Hall, and 2nd, 1817, Lucy Anne,
dau. of Sir Charles Blois, 6th Bt., of Cockfield Hall, and d. 10 Aug.
1844.   (Sources, as 4.)

IPSWICH, St. Margaret's

1. All black background
Gules three chevrons argent on a chief azure a sun in splendour or
(Fonnereau), impaling, Argent on a bend sable three chessrooks argent
(Bunbury)
Crest: A sun in splendour or   Mantling: Gules and argent
Motto: In coelo quies   Winged skull in base
For the Rev. Dr. Claudius Fonnereau, of Christ Church, Ipswich, who
m. 1728, Ann, dau. and co-heir of the Rev. William Bunbury, and d.
1 Dec. 1785.   (B.L.G. 1937 ed.; Corder's 'Christ Church', 33-4)

2. All black background
Fonnereau, impaling, Gules from a cave on the sinister side a wolf
issuant all proper (Williams)
Crest, mantling and motto: As 1.   Skull in base
For the Rev. William Fonnereau, who m. 1758, Anne, dau. and after-
wards heir of Sir Hutchins Williams, Bt., and d. 1817.   (Corder's
'Christ Church', 34)

3. All black background

Qly of six, 1st and 6th, Fonnereau, 2nd, Williams, 3rd, Bunbury, 4th,
Argent three boars' heads couped and erect sable (Booth), 5th, Argent a
fess sable issuing from the top a demi-lion rampant gules in base three
molets azure (? Oeils), impaling, Qly, 1st and 4th, Ermine a lion rampant between three dexter hands gules (Neale), 2nd and 3rd, Gules a
saltire argent between four ? pomegranates or (   )
Crest, mantling and motto: As 1.
For the Rev. Charles William Fonnereau, LL.D., R.N. (Ret.), who. m.
1791, Harriette Deborah, eldest dau. of Thomas Neale, M.D. of Freston
Tower, and d. 9 Jan. 1840, aged 75.   (B.L.G. 1937 ed., Corder's
'Christ Church'; Crisp's 'Visit.', XVII, 161)

4. Dexter background black

Qly, 1st and 4th, Fonnereau, 2nd and 3rd, Neale, impaling, Or a
chevron sable between three holly leaves vert, on a chief sable a lion
passant guardant between two fleurs-de-lys argent (Cobbold)
Crest, mantling and motto: As 1.
For William Charles Fonnereau, who m. 1832, Katherine Georgina, dau.
of John Cobbold, of Holywells, Ipswich, and d. 30 July 1855.
(B.L.G. 1937 ed.; Crisp's, 'Visit.', XVII, 162)

5. All black background

Ermine a lion rampant between three dexter hands couped at the wrist
gules (Neale)
Crest: A demi-lion rampant gules   Mantling: Gules and argent
Motto: In coelo quies   Skull in base
For Thomas Neale, LL.B., J.P., D.L., Colonel of the Ipswich Loyal
Volunteers, d. 3 Aug. 1839.   (E.A. N. and Q., IX, 232)

6. All black background

Qly, 1st and 4th, Per chevron or and azure in chief two fleurs-de-lys
gules in base five fusils conjoined in fess or each charged with an
escallops gules (Edgar), 2nd and 3rd, Or on a chief indented azure two
molets or (D'Eye)   In pretence: Or a lion rampant gules (Charlton)
Crest: A demi-ostrich with wings expanded bendy of four or and azure
in its beak a horseshoe argent   Mantling: Gules and argent
Motto: In coelo quies   Skull in base
For Mileson Edgar, of the Red House, Ipswich, who m. 1752, Elizabeth, dau. of Richard Charlton, of London, and d. 25 Mar, 1770, aged
40.   She d. 4 Apr. 1804, aged 72.   (Edgar's 'Aedes Edgarorum':
Wollaston's 'St. Margaret's', 73)
(Should be dexter black background for husband; hatchment perhaps
used for husband and subsequently for his widow)

7. All black background

Qly, 1st and 4th, Edgar, 2nd and 3rd, Charlton   In pretence: Edgar
Crest, mantling and motto: As 6.   Skull in base

For Mileson Edgar, who m. 1783, his cousin, Susannah, dau. of Robert
Edgar of Wickhambrook and Ipswich, and d. 16 June 1830, aged 68.
(B.L.G. 1900 ed.; Edgar's 'Aedes Edgarorum'; E.A. N. and Q., IX, 231)

8. Sinister background black
Qly, 1st and 4th, Edgar, 2nd and 3rd, Charlton, impaling, Argent on a
fess azure between in chief two bees flying upwards and in base a
beaver passant proper two molets of six points argent (Brickwood)
Mantling: Gules and argent   Motto: In coelo quies
Cherub's head above shield
For Mary Anne, dau. of Nathaniel Brickwood of Dulwich, who m.
1818, as his first wife, the Rev. Mileson Gery Edgar, and d. 1835.
(Sources, B.L.G., and Edgar, as 7.)

9. Dexter and sinister chief background black
Qly, 1st and 4th, Edgar, 2nd and 3rd, Gules a chevron or between three
leopards' faces argent (Edgar ancient), impaling, two coats per fess, in
chief, Brickwood, and in base, Gules a fess embattled counter-
embattled argent (Arkell)
Crest, mantling and motto: As 6.
For the Rev. Mileson Gery Edgar, who m. 1st, 1818, Mary Anne, dau.
of Nathaniel Brickwood, and 2nd, 1840, Elizabeth, dau. of William
Arkell of London, and d. 3 Aug. 1853, aged 68.   (Sources, as 8.)

IPSWICH, St. Mary Elms

1. All black background
On a lozenge surmounted by a skull
Sable three lynxes rampant guardant proper (Lynch), impaling, Sable
a chevron argent/or between three leopards' faces or (? Wentworth)
Mantling: Gules and or   Motto: Virtus periculum spernit
Probably for Athaliah, widow of William Lynch, Receiver-General for
Suffolk, who d. 1721.   She d. 12 Dec. 1722, aged 73.   (Crisp's
'Frag. Gen.', X, 92; E.A. N. and Q., IX, 266)

2. Sinister background black
Qly, 1st and 4th, Azure three helms or (Hamby), 2nd and 3rd, Azure
three cross crosslets fitchy in bend cotised or (Knatchbull)   In
pretence: Qly, 1st and 4th, Azure on a chevron argent three molets
sable (Roberts), 2nd, qly, i. and iv. Or a fess dancetty between three
cross crosslets fitchy gules (Sandys), ii. and iii. Per fess gules and azure
a tower with dome argent (Rawson), 3rd, qly i. and iv. Or on a fess
dancetty between three billets azure each charged with a lion rampant
or three bezants (Rolle), ii. and iii. Argent a chevron and in dexter
chief a trefoil slipped sable (Foote)

Crest: A falcon displayed and belled or   Mantling: Gules and argent
Motto: In coelo quies
For Elizabeth Mary, dau. and co-heir of William Roberts, who m. as his
first wife, Robert Hamby, and d. 9 Mar. 1758, aged 34.   (Tablet in
church; E.A. N. and Q., IX, 267-8)

3. Dexter background black
Dexter, as 2., impaling, Argent a chevron between three garbs banded
sable (   )
Crest and mantling: As 2.   Motto: Mors janua vitae   Skull below
shield
For Robert Hamby, who m. 1st, Elizabeth Mary, dau. and co-heir of
William Roberts, and 2nd, ?
and d. 31 Oct. 1774/5, aged 64.   (Sources, as 2)

4. Dexter background black
Qly, 1st and 4th, Sable a chevron or (   ), 2nd and 3rd, Sable three
bendlets argent a chief or   (Reed), impaling, Argent three boars'
heads erased gules (   )
Crest: (indecipherable)   Mantling: Gules and argent
Motto: In coelo quies
For James Reed, who d. 7 Dec. 1831, aged 76.   His widow, Char-
lotte, d. 23 Mar. 1835, aged 74.   (E.A. N. and Q., IX, 267-9; Farrer
MS., II)

IPSWICH, St. Peter

1. All black background
On a lozenge   Argent a cross between four roses gules barbed and
seeded proper (Trotman)   In pretence: Argent a chevron between
three boars' heads couped sable langued gules, on a chief vert three
bezants (Wardell)
Mantling: Gules and argent   Motto: In coelo quies   Cherub's
head above
For Elizabeth Wardell, who m. Robert Trotman, and d. 11 June 1821,
aged 74.   (M.I. in church; E.A. N. and Q., XII, 119)

IPSWICH, St. Stephen

1. All black background
On a lozenge   Two coats per fess; in chief, Azure an estoile within
the horns of a crescent argent (Minshull), and in base, Argent a chevron
between three hunting horns sable stringed gules (   ), both coats
impaling, Per pale or and azure a quatrefoil between in chief two

demi-lions passant guardant and in base a lion passant guardant all
counterchanged (Hammond)
Motto: Resurgam   Cherub's head above
Unidentified

2. All black background
Qly, 1st and 4th, Per chevron or and azure in chief two fleurs-de-lys
gules and in base five fusils conjoined in fess or each charged with an
escallop gules (Edgar), 2nd and 3rd, Sable a fret argent (Harrington),
impaling, Gules on each of two bars argent three mascles sable on a
canton or a leopard's face sable (Gery)
Crest: A demi-ostrich with wings expanded all bendy or and azure, in
its beak a horseshoe argent   Mantling: Gules and argent
Motto: Mors janua vitae   Skull in base
For Robert Edgar, who m. 1762, Susanna, only child of the Rev.
William Gery, Prebendary of Peterborough, and d. 6 Nov. 1778, aged
45.   (B.L.G. 2nd ed; Edgar's 'Aedes Edgarorum', 4-5)

IPSWICH, Christchurch Mansion

1. All black background
On a lozenge   Sable a fess between three mascles argent (Whitaker),
impaling, Vert a chevron embattled counter-embattled or (Hale)
Crests: to dexter of lozenge, A horse statant argent, and to sinister,
A sheaf of five arrows, points downwards argent   Skull above
A very small hatchment
For Ann Hale, who m. Charles Whitaker, Serjeant-at-law, Recorder of
Ipswich, M.P. for Ipswich, 1701, 1702.   He d. 1715, aged 73.   She
was buried at St. Nicholas, Ipswich, 30 May 1722.   (Par. Regs.;
E.A. N. and Q., X, 56; Clark's 'History of Ipswich', 236)

KEDINGTON

1. All black background
On a lozenge   Barry of ten argent and azure over all six escut-
cheons sable each charged with a lion rampant argent (Cecil),
impaling, Gules fourteen bezants, four, four, three, two, one a canton
ermine (Zouch)
Viscountess' coronet   Motto: Mors ter.. ad vita
Supporters: Two lions rampant ermine
Frame inscribed 'Ob. 12th Nov. 1691.'
For Sophia, dau. of Sir Edward Zouch, who m. as her first husband,
Edward, 1st Viscount Wimbledon, and d. 12 Nov. 1691.   (B.P. 1939
ed.; Tablet in church; Mills MS.)

2. Dexter background black

Qly, 1st and 4th, Azure a fess dancetty ermine between six cross cross-
lets argent (Barnardiston), 2nd, Argent a lion rampant double-tailed
gules (Havering), 3rd, Or two bars azure between five martlets, two,
two, one gules (Paynell), in centre chief the Badge of Ulster
In pretence: Ermine a saltire engrailed gules, on a chief gules a lion of
England (Armine)
Crest: A bittern close or among rushes proper
Mantling: Gules and argent   Motto: Je trove bien
Frame inscribed 'He obiit 4th Oct. 1669.'
For Sir Thomas Barnardiston, 1st Bt., who m. Anne, dau, and co-heir of
Sir William Armine, Bt., of co. Lincs, and d. 4 Oct. 1669.   (B.E.B.;
Mills MS.; Crisp's 'Visit. of Eng. and Wales', Notes, VII, 174)

3. All black background

On a lozenge   Barnardiston, with Badge of Ulster in chief
In pretence, and impaling, Armine
Frame inscribed 'Obit 16 Aug. 1671'
For Anne, widow of Sir Thomas Barnardiston, 1st Bt.   She d.
16 Aug. 1671.
(Sources, as 2.)

4. All black background

Qly, as 2., with Badge of Ulster in fess point, impaling, Gules a dexter
hand argent held aloft by two lions combatant or (King)
Crest, mantling and motto: As 2.   Frame inscribed 'He obt 6 Octr
1698'
For Sir Thomas Barnardiston, 2nd Bt., who m. Elizabeth, dau. and heir
of Sir Robert King, and d. 7 Oct. 1698.   (Sources, as 2.)

5. All black background (should be dexter black)

Qly of eight, 1st and 8th, Barnardiston, 2nd, Havering, 3rd, Sable a
saltire engrailed or (Franke), 4th, Sable three combs argent (Tunstall),
5th, Armine, 6th, Argent on a cross gules five molets or (   ), 7th,
Gules a fess argent between three escallops or (? Chamberlain), in
centre chief the Badge of Ulster   In pretence: Argent on two
chevrons engrailed sable six bezants (Rothwell)
Crest, mantling and motto: As 2.
Frame inscribed 'He obit 12 Novr 1700'
For Sir Thomas Barnardiston, 3rd Bt., who m. 1693/4, Anne, dau. and
co-heir of Sir Richard Rothwell, Bt. of co. Lincs, and d. 12 Nov. 1700,
aged 26.
(Sources, as 2.)

6. All black background

On a lozenge   Arms, as last, but also impaling Rothwell
Frame inscribed '14 Feb. 1701'

For Anne, widow of Sir Thomas Barnardiston.   She d. 14 Feb. 1701.
(Sources, as 2.)

7. All black background
Barnardiston, impaling, Or a bend engrailed sable charged with a
molet argent (Clark)
Crest and motto: As 2.   Frame inscribed 'He Obt 31 Octr 1704'
For Thomas Barnardiston, of London and Bury St. Edmunds, Turkey
merchant, who m. Elizabeth, dau. of John Clark of Bury, and d.
31 Oct. 1704, aged 67.   (M.I. and B.L.G. 2nd ed.; Crisp's 'Visit.',
Notes VII, 188)

8. All black background
Barnardiston, with Badge of Ulster in fess point, impaling, Gules a
cock or (Cheeke)
Crest, mantling and motto: As 2.
For Sir Robert Barnardiston, 4th Bt., who m. Elizabeth Cheeke, and d.
16 July, 1728.   (Sources, as 2., Crisp, p. 176)

9. Dexter background black
Barnardiston, with Badge of Ulster in dexter chief, impaling, Ermine on
a fess sable three eagles displayed or (Wynne)
Crest, mantling and motto: As 2.
For Sir Samuel Barnardiston, 5th Bt., who m. 1730, Catherine, dau. of
Sir Rowland Wynne, Bt., of co. Yorks, and d. 4 Feb. 1735/6, aged 55.
(Sources, as 2.; Crisp, p. 177)

10. Dexter background black
Barnardiston   In pretence: Azure a fess engrailed argent fretty sable
between three fleurs-de-lys and a bordure or (Styles)
Crest and mantling: As 2.   Motto: A cruce salus
For Nathaniel Barnardiston, of the Ryes, Sudbury, who m. 1783, as his
2nd wife, Elizabeth Joanna, only child of John Stackhouse Styles of
Islington, and d. 23 Dec. 1837, aged 82.   (Sources, as 2., Crisp,
p.190)

KELSALE

1. All black background
On a lozenge   Argent a cross engrailed sable in dexter chief an
eagle displayed gules (Trusson)   In pretence: Argent on a cross
between four frets gules a tower triple-turreted argent (Bence)
Cherub's head above
For Katherine, dau. and co-heir of the Rev. Thomas Bence, Rector
of Kelsale, who m. 1747, Gabriel Trusson, and d. 8 June 1785, aged 77.
(B.L.G. 1853 ed.; Hill's 'Regs. of Thorington')

2. All black background
Qly, 1st and 4th, Trusson, 2nd and 3rd, Bence
No crest, but winged skull above
Mantling: Gules and argent   Motto: In coelo quies
For Thomas, only son of Gabriel and Katherine Trusson, who d. unm.
27 Sept. 1809, aged 57.   (Sources, as 1.)

KERSEY

1. All black background
Azure on a chief argent three lozenge-shaped buckles tongues fesswise
azure (Thorrowgood), impaling, Argent a cross flory gules between four
escallops sable (Sampson)
Crest: A wolf's head couped argent the neck charged with a buckle as in
the arms   Mantling: Gules and argent
Motto: Virtus spernit periculum
For John Thorrowgood, of Sampson's Hall, who m. Bridget, only dau.
and heir of John Sampson of Sampson's Hall, and d. 12 June 1734,
aged 74.   (Mills MS.; Copinger, III, 182)

2. Dexter background black
Qly, 1st and 4th, Thorrowgood, 2nd and 3rd, Sampson, impaling,
Azure three close helmets or (Hamby)
Crest and mantling: As 2.   Motto: In coelo quies   No frame
For Sir Thomas Thorrowgood, who m. Katherine Hamby, and
d. 18 Dec, 1794, aged 75.   (Mills MS.; Page's 'Suffolk', 1006; Top.
et Gen. II, 157)

3. All black background
On a lozenge surmounted by a skull
Thorrowgood
Mantling: Gules and argent   Motto: In coelo quies   No frame
For Katherine Thorrowgood, who d. unm, 30 July 1802, aged 59.
Last of the family.   (Sources, as 2.)

KESGRAVE

1. All black background
Qly, 1st and 4th, Argent a chevron sable between three birds azure
beaked and legged or (Thomas), 2nd and 3rd, Argent a chevron gules
between three boars' heads erased azure langued gules (Cochrane)
Crest: A bird wings expanded azure beaked gules legged or between two
spearheads points upwards tasselled or   Mantling: Gules and argent
Motto: Virtute et labore (Cochrane)   Skull below
For George Thomas, son of George Thomas of Kesgrave and his second

wife, Anne, dau. of George Cochrane or Cockrein of Harwich, Essex,
b. at Bath, baptised there, Feb. 1791, inherited estates at Kesgrave and
Brockley, High Sheriff of Suffolk 1820, d. unm. and buried in Kesgrave
church, 7 June 1853.   (Church guide)

2. Sinister background black
Argent a chevron between three birds sable (Thomas), impaling, Argent
on a bend gules between three roundels sable three swans proper
(Clarke)
Crest: A bird wings expanded proper   Mantling: Gules and argent
Motto: In coelo quies   Skull below
For Rebecca, dau. of the Rev. John Clarke, of Woodbridge, who m. as
his first wife, George Thomas of Kesgrave. She d. and was buried at
Kesgrave 12 Oct. 1770.   (Church guide)
(Details of this hatchment were recorded when the survey began in
1952, but it has since disappeared)

LONG MELFORD

1. All black background
Qly of twenty-one, 1st, Argent six lions rampant, three, two, one sable
(Savage), 2nd, Argent seven mascles conjoined three, three, one gules
(Braybrooke), 3rd, Gules a chevron between three martlets argent
(Walkington), 4th, Argent a pale lozengy sable (Daniel), 5th, Or three
lozenges azure (Baggeley), 6th, Or a fess sable (Vernon), 7th Qly argent
and gules in the 2nd and 3rd a fret or (Dutton), 8th, Or a cross flory
sable (Swinnerton), 9th, Gules a cross ermine (Beke), 10th, Sable a fess
humetty argent (Bostock), 11th, Azure three garbs or (Blundeville),
12th, Azure two bars or (Venables), 13th, Qly gules and or (? Dutton),
14th, Azure between the horns of a crescent an estoile or (Minshull),
15th, Sable a bend engrailed between six billets argent, a crescent for
difference (Alington), 16th, Gules three covered cups argent (Butler),
17th, Azure six martlets three, two, one and a canton argent
(Arundell), 18th, Per fess or and sable a pale and three griffins' heads
erased counterchanged (Gardner), 19th, Argent fretty and a canton
sable (Middleton), 20th, Gules a chevron between three griffins' heads
erased argent (Cordell), 21st, Azure a chevron between three lions
passant guardant or (Webb), impaling, Qly of twelve, 1st, Argent three
cinquefoils gules (Darcy), 2nd, Gules seven cross crosslets three, one,
three or, that in fess point within an orle or (Baltram or Bertram), 3rd,
Argent a fess between six oak leaves gules (Fitzlangley), 4th, Argent
a fess sable ermined argent cotised sable (Harleston), 5th, Argent a
chevron sable, in dexter chief an annulet sable for difference (Wanton),
6th, Gules a goat salient argent (Bardwell), 7th, Qly argent and gules
the 1st quarter charged with an eagle displayed vert (Pakenham), 8th,
Argent three pallets wavy gules (Garnon), 9th, Sable out of a maunch
argent a hand holding a fleur-de-lys or (Creke), 10th, Argent a chief

indented gules (Hengrave), 11th, blank, 12th, Argent three cinquefoils
gules (Darcy)
Viscount's coronet   Crests: Dexter, From a ducal coronet or a lion's
gamb sable armed gules   Sinister, A demi-virgin, vested gules, holding
in her dexter hand three flowers gules   Mantling, to dexter, Azure
and ermine, and to sinister, Gules and ermine   Motto: A te pro te
Supporters: Dexter, A unicorn argent   Sinister, A stag ermine
Inscribed on frame 'Viscount Savage 1635'
For Thomas, 1st Viscount Savage, who m. Elizabeth, dau. and co-heir
of Thomas, Lord Darcy, and d. 20 Nov. 1635, aged c. 49.   (B.E.P.;
Proc. S.I.A. XXVI, 214-19)

2. All black background
Or on a chief sable three lions' heads erased or (Richardson), impaling,
Azure three storks rising proper (Gibson)
Crest: Out of a ducal coronet or a mailed arm lying fessways holding a
sword erect, on the blade a wreath tied all proper
Mantling: Gules and argent   Motto: Resurgam
Inscribed on frame 'Thos. Richardson, Esqr 1818'
For Thomas Richardson, of Long Melford, who m. Jane, dau. of
William Gibson, and d. 1818, aged 89.   She d. aged 76, and was
buried at Mendlesham, 25 Jan, 1809.   (Partridge's 'Suff. Church-
yard Inscriptions', 13, 89)

3. All black background
On a lozenge   Qly, 1st and 4th, Argent a lion passant gules between
two bars sable charged with three bezants, two and one, in chief three
stags' heads cabossed sable (Parker), 2nd and 3rd, Azure a chevron
between three griffins segreant or (? Griffinhoofe)
In pretence: Azure a chevron between three cinquefoils argent (Service)
Mantling: Gules and argent   Motto: Sum quod eris   Scallop shell
above
Inscribed on frame 'Elizabeth Parker 1833'
For Elizabeth, elder dau. and co-heir of Robert Service, of London,
who m. John Oxley Parker, of Chelmsford, and d. 14 Jan. 1833, aged
57.   (Farrer MS., I, 58, 67; B.L.G. 1900)

4. All black background
On a lozenge   Or three piles in point piercing a human heart gules
(Logan)
In pretence: Azure a chevron between three cinquefoils argent (Service)
Mantling: Gules and argent   Motto: Sum quod eris   Cherub's head
above
Inscribed on frame 'Nancy, Daughter of Robt. Service, Esqr. Widow of
Hart Logan, Esqr. Died 1845'.
For Nancy, Sister of Elizabeth Service (*see* 3.), who m. 1818, R. H.
Logan, merchant of London, and d. 1845.   (Proc. S.I.A., II. 71)

5. All black background
On a lozenge   Ermine on a chief gules three lions rampant or
(Oliver)
In pretence: Or on a chief sable three lions' heads erased or
(Richardson)
Mantling: Azure and argent   Motto: Resurgam   Cherub's head
above
Inscribed on frame 'Harriet Oliver, Ww. died Jany 7th 1834. A
Benefractress to this parish'
For Harriet, dau. of Thomas Richardson (*see* 2) who m. 1st, Philip
Hamond (*see* Hawkedon 3) and 2nd, John Oliver, (*see* Hawkedon 1),
and d. 7 Jan. 1834.   (Copinger, V, 245; Parker's 'Melford', 196)

6. All black background
On a lozenge   Qly, 1st and 4th, Argent three lozenges gules
(Pitcairn), 2nd and 3rd, Argent an eagle displayed sable (Ramsay),
all within a bordure ermine (for Pitcairn)   In pretence: Per bend
or and sable a cross potent counterchanged (Almack)
Mantling: Gules and argent   Cherub's head above
Inscribed on frame 'Elizabeth, Daur of Wm. Almack, Esqr. Widow of
Dr David Pitcairn. Died 1844'

7. Sinister background black
Sable a stag's head cabossed or between two flaunches argent (Parker),
impaling, Gules three roundels argent each charged with a squirrel gules
(Cresswell); in centre chief the Badge of Ulster
Mantling: Gules and argent   Motto: In coelo quies   Cherub's head
above
Frame inscribed 'Lady Parker 1807'
For Bridget, dau. of William Cresswell, who m. 1766, Sir Henry Parker,
6th Bt. of Melford Hall, and was buried at Melford 29 Jan. 1807, aged
62.   (B.P. 1891 ed.; Farrer's 'Portraits in W. Suff. Houses', 255)

8. All black background
Parker, with Badge of Ulster in chief
Crest: A dexter arm erect sleeved azure cuffed and slashed argent, in the
hand proper a stag's attire gules   Mantling: Gules and argent
Motto: In coelo quies
Frame inscribed 'Sir Wm. Parker, Bart. 1830'
For Sir William Parker, 7th Bt., who d. unm. 21 Apr. 1830   (B.P.
1891 ed.)

9. All black background
Qly, 1st and 4th, Parker, 2nd and 3rd, Azure a chevron between three
lozenges or (Hyde) in centre chief the Badge of Ulster
Crest and mantling: As 8.   Motto: Fideli certa merces
Inscribed on frame 'Sir Hyde Parker, Bart. 1856'

For Sir Hyde Parker, 8th Bt., who d. unm. 21 Mar. 1856, aged 71.
(B.P. 1891 ed.; Farrer's 'Portraits', 258-9)

MARLESFORD

1. All black background
Azure an eagle displayed or beaked gules (Shuldham), impaling, Or
two chevrons between three fleurs-de-lys gules (Barber)
Crest: A griffin passant argent beaked gules   Mantle: Gules and
argent
Motto: Post nubila phoebus
For William Shuldham, of Marlesford Hall, who m. 1786, Mary, dau. of
Robert Barber of Boyton, and d. 1845, aged 102.   (B.L.G. 1853 ed.;
Top. and Gen., II, 502)

MARTLESHAM

1. Dexter background black
Or a fess between six lions' heads erased gules (Goodwin), impaling,
Argent three bendlets gules on a canton azure a spur leathered or
(Knights)
Crest: A griffin sejant wings expanded sable gutty or
Mantling: Gules and argent   Motto: Mors janua vitae
For John Goodwin, of Martlesham and Grundisburgh, who m. Mary,
dau. and co-heir of Thomas Knights, and d. 22 Mar, 1742, aged 48.
(Muskett's 'Suffolk Manorial Families', I, 214; E.A. N. and Q., XIII,
357; Church guide)

2. All black background
On a lozenge   Goodwin impaling Knights
Mantling: Gules and argent   Motto: Mors janua vitae
Skull and crossbones above
For Mary, widow of John Goodwin.   She d. 12 Jan. 1769, aged 68.
(Sources, as 1.)

3. Dexter background black
Goodwin, impaling, Argent a fess gules between three jackboots sable
(Tramell)
Crest, and mantling: As 1.   Motto: In coelo quies   Skull below
For John Goodwin, who m. 1743, Grace Tramell, and d.s.p. 3 Jan.
1758, aged 34.   (Sources, as 1.)

4. All black background
Qly, 1st Goodwin, 2nd, Azure three swords palewise, the centre one
point in chief the others in base proper (? Docker), 3rd, Per chevron

or and azure, in chief two fleurs-de-lys gules and in base five fusils
conjoined in fess or each charged with an escallop gules (Edgar), 4th,
Gules a chevron argent charged with three bars gemel sable
(Throckmorton)
Crest and mantling: As 1.
A small hatchment, c. 2ft. x 2ft.
For William Goodwin, son of John Goodwin, of Ipswich, by his wife
Mary, dau. of Henry Edgar of Dennington, by Bridget Docker.   He d.
1663/4.   (Church guide, 1951 ed.)

5. Sinister background black
Or a leopard's face azure between three eagles' heads erased gules all
within a bordure gules bezanty (Sharpe), impaling, Goodwin
Motto: En Dieu est tout   Two cherubs' heads above
For Anne, dau. and co-heir of William Goodwin of Woodbridge, who m.
1819, the Rev. Charles Sharpe Sharpe, and d. 21 Apr. 1843, aged 52.
(Sources, as 1)

6. All black background
On a lozenge
Or on a chevron gules three roses argent, a canton gules (Capper)
Mantling: Gules and argent
For Mary, dau. of the Rev. Francis Capper, Rector of Earl and Monk
Soham, b. 1770, d. unm. 19 Nov. 1837.   (Misc. Gen. et Her. 4th
series, II, 80-1; Church guide)

MELTON (old church)

1. Dexter background black
Or a leopard's face between three eagles' heads erased azure all within
a bordure invected gules bezanty (Sharpe), impaling, Or three pallets
azure, on a chief gules three martlets or (Martin)
Crest: A wolf's head erased per pale or and azure
Mantling: Gules and argent, lined and tasselled or
Motto: En Dieu est tout
For Charles Thomas Rissowe, later Sharpe, who m. 1792, Eleanor, dau.
of Peter Martin of London, and d. 1821.   (B.L.G. 1853 ed.)

2. All black background
On a lozenge
Sharpe impaling Martin (the martlets argent and a crescent argent for
difference)
All on a mantle gules and ermine, lined and tasselled or
For Eleanor, widow of Charles Thomas Sharpe.   She d.
(B.L.G. 1853 ed.)

MENDLESHAM

1. Sinister background black
Or three lions rampant gules (Cresacre), impaling, Barry of six argent
and sable a canton ermine (Marshall)
Motto: In coelo quies   Cherub's head above
Unidentified

NORTH COVE

1. All black background
Gules a saltire cotised or between four fleurs-de-lys argent (Farr),
impaling, Per pale argent and sable a chevron between three talbots
passant counterchanged, on a chief gules three leopards' heads or (Gooch)
Crest: A griffin's head erased argent langued gules
Mantling: Gules and argent   Motto: Spes mea in Deo
For Thomas Farr, of Beccles, who m. Georgiana, youngest dau. of Sir
Thomas Gooch, 3rd Bt., and d. 9 June 1850, aged 87.   (B.P. 1939
ed.: E.A. N. and Q., IV, 265; Suckling, I, 50; Crisp's 'Visitation',
X, 140)

OUSDEN

1. Dexter background black
Gules six fleurs-de-lys, three, two, one argent (Ireland), impaling, Sable
a fess between three fleurs-de-lys argent (Welby)
Crest: A dove close holding in the beak an olive branch proper
Mantling: Gules and argent   Motto: Resurgam
For Thomas James Ireland, of Ousden Hall, who m. 1829, Elizabeth,
dau. of Sir William Earle Welby, Bt. of co. Lincs, and d. 2 July 1863,
aged 71.   (B.L.G. 1853 ed.; Church tablet)

2. Dexter background black
Argent a bend gules between two bendlets sable (Frampton), impaling,
Azure a crescent between three molets argent (Arbuthnot)
Crest: A greyhound sejant argent collared gules   Motto: Resurgemus
For the Rev. Thomas Frampton, D.D., Rector of Ousden, who d.
18 June 1803, aged 78; his widow, Mary Day, d. 30 Jan. 1808, aged 60.
(Church tablet: 'Bury and Environs', 259)

PAKENHAM

1. Dexter background black
Argent on a mount vert a hawk rising proper belled or, in chief three
molets gules (Discipline)   In pretence: Qly, 1st and 4th, Argent a
chevron between three mascles gules (Spring), 2nd, Sable a crescent
between two molets in pale argent (Jermyn), 3rd, Argent a chevron
sable between three oak leaves vert (Trelawney)
Crest: A demi-hawk displayed proper in the beak a cinquefoil slipped
argent   Mantling: Gules and argent
Frame decorated with emblems of mortality
For Thomas Discipline, of Bury and Pakenham Hall, who m. Merelina,
dau. and co-heir of Sir Thomas Spring, 3rd, Bt. of Pakenham, and d.
18 Apr. 1752.   (Misc. Gen. et Her. 4th Ser., II, 116; Copinger, VI,
307)

2. All black background
On a lozenge   Arms: As 1.
Cherub's head above, and crowned and winged skull below
Frame painted with cherubs' heads in corners, banks of clouds on sides
For Merelina, widow of Thomas Discipline.   She d. 6 Nov. 1761.
(Sources, as 1)

PALGRAVE

1. Dexter background black
Argent two bars gules in chief a crescent or for difference (Martin),
impaling, Qly, 1st and 4th, Per pale sable and gules a unicorn passant
or, on a chief argent three gillyflowers proper, the centre one surmounted by a sword and key in saltire or (Flower), 2nd and 3rd, Or
ermined sable a roundel gules between three swans' heads and necks
erased sable (? Squire)
Crest: An estoile of six points or   No mantling or motto
For the Rev. Charles Martin, Rector of Palgrave, who m. Clarissa, dau.
of Sir Charles Flower, 1st Bt., and his wife, Ann Squire.   He d.
31 Jan. 1864, aged 75.   (Farrer MS., I, 471)

PARHAM

1. All black background
Or on a chevron between three wolves' heads erased sable three
leopards' faces or (White)   In pretence (a lozenge): Argent on a
chevron between three Cornish choughs proper three leopards' faces or
(Corrance)
Mantling: Gules and argent   Skull and crossbones below

For Mary, dau. of Major John Corrance, who m. 1782, her cousin,
Snowden White, M.D. of Nottingham, and was bur. at Dawlish, Devon,
21 Dec. 1836, aged 86.   (B.L.G. 1853 ed.: Farrer MS., II, 29)

2. All black background
On a lozenge.   Argent three pallets sable each charged with three
leopards' faces or (Long)   In pretence: Corrance
Skull below
For Elizabeth, dau. of Clemence Corrance, M.P., of Parham, who m.
Israel Long, of Dunston, co. Norfolk, and d. 30 Dec. 1792, aged 84.
(B.L.G. 1853 ed.)

POLSTEAD

1. All black background
Vert a griffin passant and a chief or (Brand)   In pretence: Azure
three cinquefoils argent (Vincent)
Crest: A demi-griffin segreant holding a battleaxe or
Mantling: Gules and argent, cords and tassels or
For Jacob Brand (aged 14 in 1664) who m. Judith, dau. of Sir William
Vincent, and d.   (Vincent mon. in church; 'Vis. of Suffolk',
1664-8)

2. All black background
Brand, the field azure
Crest: As 1.   Mantling: Gules and argent   Motto: In coelo quies
Unidentified

3. All black background
Qly, 1st and 4th, Brand, the field sable, 2nd and 3rd, Sable three
quatrefoils argent (Vincent)   In pretence: Sable on a chevron or
between three griffins' heads erased argent three molets sable (Beale)
Crest: A demi-griffin holding a battleaxe or   Mantling: Gules and
argent
For Jacob Brand, who m. Jane, dau. and co-heir of Bartholomew Beale,
and d.   (Copinger, I, 181, pencilled notes)

4. Dexter background black
Brand, as 3., impaling, Azure three bars wavy ermine, on a chief or a
demi-lion rampant issuant sable (Smyth)
Crest: A griffin sejant holding a battleaxe or   Mantling: As 3.
Motto: In coelo quies
For William Beale Brand, who m. Anna Mirabella Henrietta, dau. of
Sir Robert Smyth, 2nd Bt., of Isfield, Sussex, and d. 1799.
(Copinger, I, 181; Betham's 'Baronetage', III, 182)

5. All black background
On a lozenge   Brand, as 3.   In pretence: Qly, 1st, Sable two bars wavy ermine, on a chief or a demi-lion rampant sable (Smyth), 2nd, Bendy of six argent and sable a canton ermine (Shirley), 3rd, Argent a chevron sable between three mascles gules (Ashton), 4th, Ermine a cross flory gules (Gower)
Mantling and motto: As 4.   Cherub's head above
For Anna Mirabella Henrietta, widow of William Beale Brand.   She d. 1814.   (Sources, as 4)

POSLINGFORD

1. Dexter background black
Argent on a chevron sable nine bezants, in dexter chief a crescent sable for difference (Severne), impaling, Or on a fess azure four crescents argent (Yelloly)
Crest: A cinquefoil or   Mantling: Gules and argent
Motto: Virtus proestantior auro
For Samuel Amy Severne, of Poslingford Park, who m. 2nd, 1864, Sarah Boddicott, dau. of John Yelloly, of Cavendish Hall, and d. 25 Jan. 1865.   (B.L.G. 1852 ed.; Suckling's 'A Forgotten Past', 125-30)

2. Sinister background black
Per pale or and gules a chevron counterchanged (Weston).   In pretence: Per pale indented or and gules a chevron between three roundels all counterchanged (   )
Motto: Bene exerce facultatem tuam   Cherub's head above
For Mary, wife of Col. Thomas Weston, of Shadowbush.   She d. 5 Mar. 1839, aged 64.   (Proc. S.I.A., VIII, 254)

3. All black background
Arms: As 2.
Crest: An eagle's head erased argent   Mantling: Gules and argent
Motto: In coelo quies
For Col. Thomas Weston, of Shadowbush, who d. 27 Nov. 1843, aged 80.   (Source, as 2., 253)

REDGRAVE

1. Dexter background black
Qly, 1st and 4th, Gules on a chief argent two molets sable (Bacon), 2nd and 3rd, Barry of six or and azure over all a bend gules (Quaplode), in fess point the Badge of Ulster, impaling, Argent a fess between three cross crosslets fitchy gules (Crane)

Crest: A boar statant ermine, armed, hoofed and crined or
Mantling: Gules and argent
For Sir Edmund Bacon, 4th Bt., who m. Elizabeth, dau. and co-heiress
of Sir Robert Crane, Bt. of Chilton and d. 12 Sept. 1685, aged 52.
(B.P. 1891 ed.; tablet in church)

2. All black background
Qly, as 1. with Badge of Ulster in fess point, impaling, Gules three
garbs within a bordure engrailed or (Kemp)
Crest: A boar passant ermine, armed hoofed and crined or
Motto: Mediocria firma
For Sir Edmund Bacon, 6th Bt., who m. 1712, Letitia, dau. of Sir
Robert Kemp, 3rd, Bt., and d. June 1755.   (B.P. 1891 ed.; Hitchin-
Kemp's 'Kemp and Kempe Families', part II, 48)

3. All black background
On a lozenge   Qly, 1st and 4th, Gules on a chief argent two molets
pierced sable (Bacon), 2nd and 3rd, Or two bars azure over all a bend
gules (Quaplode)
Motto: Mediocria firma
Probably for Elizabeth, youngest dau. of Sir Edmund Bacon and his
wife Letitia Kemp; she was buried at Redgrave, 10 May 1738.
(B.P. 1891 ed.; church register)

4. Dexter background black
Argent on a bend engrailed sable three fleurs-de-lys argent (Holt),
impaling, Ermine on a chief gules three owls argent (Cropley)
Crest: A forearm sleeved per pale argent and sable cuffed argent, in the
hand proper a pheon sable   Mantling: Gules and argent
Motto: Que serra serra
For Sir John Holt, Lord Chief Justice, who m. Anne, sister of Sir John
Cropley, Bt., and d.s.p. 1709.   (B.L.G. 1853 ed.; Copinger, I, 318)

5. Dexter background black
Holt, impaling, Azure three keys palewise wards upwards argent in fess
point an estoile or (Ballow)
Crest and mantling: As 4., but pheon argent   Motto: Mors janua vitae
For Rowland Holt, who m. Prisca, dau. of Augustus Ballow of Norwich,
and d. 11 Feb. 1718/9.   (Sources, as 4.)

6. All black background
On a lozenge   Arms: As 5.
Cherub's head above
For Prisca, widow of Rowland Holt.   She d.   (Sources, as 4.)

7. Dexter background black
Holt, impaling, Argent two bars and in chief three molets gules
(Washington)

Crest and mantling: As 4. Winged skull and crossbones in base
For Rowland Holt, who m. Elizabeth Washington, and d. 25 July 1739,
aged 41. (Sources, as 4.)

8. All black background
Holt arms only
Crest and mantling: As 5. Motto: Che sara sara
For Rowland Holt, M.P. for Suffolk, 1759, who d. unm. 12 July 1786.
(Sources, as 4.)

9. Dexter background black
Holt, impaling, Gules two chevronels ermine between three eagles
displayed or (Parson)
Crest and mantling: As 5. Motto: Che sara sara
For Thomas Holt, who m. 1786, Frances Parson, of Parndon, Essex,
and d.s.p. 21 Aug. 1799, aged 68. (Sources, as 4.)

10. Dexter background black
Per pale argent and gules on a chevron invected between three wolves'
heads erased three molets all counterchanged (Wilson), impaling, Argent
a chevron between three escallops sable (Pollard)
Crest: On a cloud proper a crescent gules flaming or
Mantling: Gules and argent Motto: Resurgam
A trophy of arms, anchors and ensigns behind and flanking shield
For George Wilson, Admiral of the Red. who m. 1801, Catherine, dau.
of John Pollard of Ewell, Surrey, and d. 3 Mar. 1826. (B.L.G.
1952 ed.; Copinger, I, 319)

11. All black background
Wilson, impaling, Ermine on a canton gules an escutcheon argent
(Surtees)
Crest, mantling and motto: As 10.
For George St. Vincent Wilson, who m. 1834, Matilda Louisa, dau. of
the Rev. John Surtees, Prebenday of Bristol, and d. Dec. 1852.
(Sources, as 10.)

12. Dexter background black
Wilson, impaling, Azure a dolphin naiant argent (James)
Crest and motto: As 10. Trophy of arms, etc.: As 10.
For George Holt Wilson, D.L., J.P., High Sheriff, 1877, who m. 1865,
Lucy Caroline, eldest dau. of William Edward James of Barrock Park,
Cumberland, and d. 3 Sept. 1924, aged 88. (Sources, as 10.)

13. Dexter background black
Wilson, impaling, Azure three celestial crowns argent (Powell)
Crests: Dexter, as 10., the crescent argent Sinister, a bugle horn
argent

Mantling: Gules and argent
Mottoes: Dexter, Resurgam   Sinister, Stand fast
Inscribed on frame: George Rowland Holt Wilson obit June 17, 1929
For George Rowland Holt Wilson, J.P., who m. 1898, Gwendoline,
eldest dau. of the Rev. Thomas Powell, of Dorstone, co. Hereford, and
d. 17 June 1929.   (B.L.G. 1952 ed.)

RUSHBROOKE

1. All black background
Qly, 1st and 4th, Sable a fess between three roses or barbed vert (Rushbrooke), 2nd and 3rd, qly i. and iv. Argent a fess sable ermined argent
cotised sable between three martlets sable (Edwards), ii. and iii. Per pale
azure and gules three lions rampant argent (Herbert), impaling, Qly, 1st
and 4th, Ermine on a chief embattled gules three roses or (Grubb), 2nd
and 3rd, Argent two bendlets engrailed sable over all a label of three
points gules (Ratcliffe)
Crest: A lion sejant in his mouth a rose or
Mantling: Gules and argent   Motto: Fluminis ritu ferimur
For Robert Rushbrooke, of Rushbrook Park, who m. 1778, Mary
Grubb, of Horsendon, Bucks, and d. at Canterbury, 1829.
(B.L.G. 1853 ed.; Hervey's 'Rushbrook Parish Registers', 392-3)

SANTON DOWNHAM

1. Dexter background black
Qly, 1st and 4th, Azure three sinister gauntlets or (Vane), 2nd and 3rd,
qly i. and iv. Qly France and England, ii. Scotland, iii. Ireland, over all
a baton sinister counter compony ermine and azure (Fitzroy), impaling,
Or six annulets, three, two, one sable (Lowther)
Duke's coronet   Crests: Dexter, A dexter gauntlet brandishing a
sword proper   Sinister, On a chapeau gules and ermine a lion passant
guardant or collared compony ermine and azure, ducally crowned azure
Supporters: Dexter, A lion or collared compony ermine and azure
ducally crowned azure   Sinister, A greyhound argent collared
compony ermine and azure   Motto: Nec temere nec timide
For William John Frederick, 3rd Duke of Cleveland, who m. 1815,
Caroline, 4th dau. of William, 1st Earl of Lonsdale, and d. 6 Sept.
1864.   (B.P. 1891 ed.)
(There is an identical hatchment at Raby Castle, Durham)

SHELLEY

1. Dexter background black
Sable on a pile argent a caltrap sable (Kerridge)   In pretence, and
impaling, Sable three church bells argent a canton ermine (Porter)
Crest: On a mount vert a caltrap sable   Mantling: Gules and argent
Motto: Mors janua vitae
For Thomas Kerridge, of Shelley Hall, who m. Jane, dau. and heir of
Richard Porter of Framlingham, and d. Apr. 1743.   (E.A. N. and Q.,
VI, 90-1; Copinger, VI, 82)
(His widow's hatchment is at Framlingham)

2. All black background
On a lozenge surmounted by a skull
Kerridge, impaling, Azure two lions rampant guardant combatant
argent (Garrard)
Frame painted with skulls and crossbones
For Mary, dau. of Sir Thomas Garrard, Bt., who m. Samuel Kerridge
and d.   (E.A. N. and Q., VI, 90; Farrer MS., II, 157-8)

SOMERSHAM

1. Dexter background black
Gules on a chief argent two molets sable (Bacon), impaling, Argent a
lion passant reguardant sable between ten cross crosslets fitchy gules
(? Bawle)
Crest: A boar passant ermine tusked or   Mantling: Gules and argent
Motto: In Deo spes
Unidentified

SOTTERLEY

1. Dexter background black
Qly, 1st and 4th, Azure three leopards' heads argent (Barne), 2nd and
3rd, Argent a chevron azure between three Cornish choughs proper
(Ashthorpe), impaling, Gules two bars gemel and a chief argent (Thorn-
hill)
No crest or mantling   Motto: In coelo quies   Two cherubs' heads
above and skull in base
For Miles Barne, of Sotterley, M.P., who m. 2nd, Mary, dau. of George
Thornhill, of co. Hunts, and d. 20 Dec. 1780.   (B.L.G. 1853 ed.;
Suckling, I, 95)

2. All black background
On a lozenge surmounted by a cherub's head   Arms: As 1.
Motto: Resurgam
For Mary, eldest dau. of George Thornhill, widow of Miles Barne.
She d.   (Sources, as 1.)

3. All black background
Qly, 1st and 4th, Barne, 2nd, Ashthorpe, 3rd, Argent on a chevron
azure three fleurs-de-lys argent (Elwick)
Crest: An eagle sable ducally gorged or   Mantling: Gules and argent
Motto: In coelo quies
For Miles Barne, M.P., son of Miles Barne (No. 1.) by his 1st wife,
Elizabeth, dau. of Nathaniel Elwick, of Kent.   He d. unm. 8 Sept.
1825.   (Sources, as 1.)

4. All black background
On a lozenge   Qly, 1st and 4th, Azure three leopards' heads or
(Barne), 2nd and 3rd, Ashthorpe, impaling, Qly, 1st and 4th, Azure a
cock or (Boucherett), 2nd and 3rd, Sable a fess or between three asses
argent (Ayscough)
For Mary, dau. of Ayscough Boucherett, of Willingham, Lincs, who
m. 1798, Lt.-Col. Michael Barne, M.P., and d. 11 Dec. 1858, aged 93.
(Sources, as 1; Crisp's 'Visit. of Eng. and Wales', VII, 158-9)

SOUTHWOLD

1. Dexter background black
Vert on a chevron between three stags trippant or three trefoils slipped
gules (Robinson), impaling, Argent on a cross azure between four
Cornish choughs proper five passion nails or (Alefounder)
Crest: A stag's head erased or   Mantling: Gules and argent
Motto: Resurgam   Skull in base
For John Robinson, who m. Elizabeth Alefounder, and d. 24 May
1802, aged 70.   (Church booklet)

STANNINGFIELD

The following three hatchments were recorded in 1953 in the Rectory
coach house. They were in very poor condition and have since been
destroyed.

1. All black background
Argent six chessrooks sable (Rookwood)   In pretence: Argent a sun
in splendour gules (For Hanford)   Also impaling two coats per fess,
in chief, Argent a chevron between three mascles sable (Martin), in
base, Argent a sun in splendour gules (for Hanford)

Crest: A chessrook argent   Mantling: (not noted)   Motto:
Constantia
Inscribed on frame: Thomas Rookwood, Esq. 1726
For Thomas Rookwood, of Coldham Hall, who m. 1st, Tamworth, dau.
of Sir Roger Martin, of Long Melford, and 2nd, Dorothy Maria, dau. of
Compton Hanford, of Woollas Hall, co. Worcs, and d. 21 Aug. 1726.
(E.A. Misc. 1924, 30-6; Gage's 'Thingoe', 205; Betham's 'Baronetage',
II, 408; Mills MS., II, 553)

2. **All black background**
Qly azure and argent a saltire gules (Gage)   In pretence: Rookwood,
with crescent for cadency
Crest: A ram passant argent armed or   Mantling: (not noted)
Inscribed on frame: John Gage, Esq. 1728
For John Gage, who m. Elizabeth, only dau. and heir of Thomas Rook-
wood, of Coldham Hall, and d. 20 July 1728.   (Sources, as 1)

3. **Sinister background black**
Qly, 1st and 4th, Gage, 2nd and 3rd, Rookwood, over all the Badge of
Ulster   In pretence: Argent three bendlets gules on a canton azure a
spur or (Knight)
Crest: (indecipherable)   Mantling: (not noted)
Motto: Courage sans peure
Inscription on frame: Lucy, Lady Gage 1781
For Lucy, dau. of William Knight, of Kingerby, Lincs, who m. Sir
Thomas Rookwood Gage, 5th Bt., and d. 3 Sept. 1781.   (B.P. 1875
ed.)

STONHAM ASPALL

1. **Sinister background black**
Qly, 1st and 4th, Gules a fess engrailed within a bordure engrailed
ermine (Acton), 2nd and 3rd, Argent a fess between in chief two
roundels and in base a martlet sable (Lee), impaling, Per bend or and
sable three griffins' heads erased counterchanged, on a chief argent a
fleur-de-lys between two roses gules barbed vert (Rycroft)
Mantling: Gules and argent   Motto: Resurgam   Cherub's head
above
For Penelope, dau. of the Rev. Sir Richard Nelson Rycroft, 1st Bt., of
Kent, who m. 1791, as his second wife, Nathaniel Lee Acton of Livermere Park, and d. 1819.
(B.P. 1949 ed.; Copinger, II, 260; Colvile's 'History of the Colvile
Family', 184)

2. **All black background**
Qly, 1st and 4th, Acton (fess not engrailed), 2nd and 3rd, Lee, impaling, two coats per fess, in chief, Argent a fess wavy azure between three wolves' heads erased gules (Miller), and in base, Rycroft
Crest: An arm in armour embowed holding a sword argent enfiled thereon a boar's head sable   Mantling:Gules and argent
Motto: Resurgam
For Nathaniel Lee Acton, of Livermere Park, who m. 1st, 1787, Susanna, dau. of Sir Thomas Miller, 5th Bt., and 2nd, 1791, Penelope, dau. of the Rev. Sir Richard Nelson Rycroft, 1st Bt., and d. 1 Jan. 1836.   (Proc. S.I.A. XXX, 272-4)

STOWLANGTOFT

1. **Sinister background black**
Gules a bend between six unicorns' heads erased argent, in chief the Badge of Ulster (Wombwell)   In pretence: Qly, 1st, Argent a chevron gules between three fleurs-de-lys azure (Belasyse), 2nd, Argent a pale engrailed plain cotised sable (Belasyse), 3rd, Argent a fess gules between three roundels sable (   ), 4th, Or an escutcheon within an orle of martlets three, two, two, sable (Brownlow)
Motto: In well beware   Two cherubs' heads above
For Lady Anne Belasyse, dau. and co-heir of Henry, 2nd Earl of Fauconberg, who m. 1791, as his 1st wife, Sir George Wombwell, 2nd Bt., and d. 7 July 1808.   (B.P. 1891 ed.)

2. **Sinister background black**
Sable a wolf rampant or, in chief a fleur-de-lys or between two bezants (Wilson), impaling, Qly, 1st and 4th, Or a lion rampant within a double tressure flory-counter-flory gules (Maitland), 2nd, Or a cross sable charged with five crescents argent (Ellis), 3rd, Argent three bars and a canton gules (Fuller)
Mantling: Gules and argent   Motto: Atet at prope est
Cherubs' heads at top corners of shield, blue lover's knot above
For Mary Fuller, dau. of Ebenezer Fuller Maitland, of Park Place, Henley, who m. 1824, as his 1st wife, Henry Wilson, and d. before 1839. (B.L.G. 1900 ed.)

3. **All black background**
Sable a wolf rampant or on a chief or a pale sable charged with a fleur-de-lys argent between two roundels sable (Wilson), impaling two coats per fess, in chief, Maitland, and in base, Per pale or and gules three leopards' faces counterchanged (Welford)
Crest: A demi-wolf or, the sinister paw resting on a roundel sable charged with a fleur-de-lys or   Mantling: Sable and or
Motto: Wil sone wil

For Joseph Wilson of Stowlangtoft Hall, who m. 1st, 1792, Mary Anne, dau. of Robert Maitland, of Greenwich, and 2nd, 1800, Emma, dau. of John Welford, of Blackheath, and d. 1851. She also d. 1851. (B.L.G. 1900 ed.)

STOWMARKET

1. Dexter background black
Argent two chevronels azure within a bordure engrailed gules (Tyrell), impaling, Argent on a saltire sable five escallops argent, a chief indented sable charged with a lion passant argent (Baker)
Crest: A boar's head couped and erect argent, out of the mouth a peacock's tail proper   Mantling: Gules and argent   Motto: Resurgam
Supporters: Two tigers reguardant proper   Leopard's face below shield
For the Rev. Charles Tyrell, of Gipping Hall, Rector of Thurston, who m. 1774, Elizabeth, dau. of Edmund Baker, of Stow Upland, and d. 1811, aged 70.
(Bright's 'Brights of Suffolk', 225-6, 229: E.A. Misc. 1929, 82-3)

STUTTON

1. Sinister background black
Ermine a millrind sable in centre chief a molet sable for difference (Mills), impaling, Azure a fess dancetty ermine between six cross crosslets argent (Barnardiston)
Mantling: Gules and argent   Motto: Confido   Cherub's head above
For Anne, 2nd dau. of Nathaniel Barnardiston, of the Ryes, Sudbury, who m. 1815, as his 1st wife, the Rev. Thomas Mills, Rector of Stutton, and d. 7 May, 1827, aged 31.   (B.L.G. 1853 ed.; Crisp's 'Parish of Stutton')

SUDBOURNE

1. All black background
Qly of sixteen, 1st, Argent a fess and in chief three roundels gules (Devereux), 2nd, Argent a cross engrailed gules between four water bougets sable (Bourchier), 3rd, Qly France and England within a bordure argent (Thomas of Woodstock), 4th, Azure a bend argent cotised or between six lions rampant or (Bohun), 5th, Gules two bends that in chief or and that in base argent (Fitzwalter), 6th, Per pale or and gules an escarbuncle sable (Mandeville), 7th, Gules a fess argent between ten billets or (Lovaine), 8th, Argent a fess and a canton gules (Widville),

9th, Argent a saltire gules fretty or (Crophull), 10th, Or a fret gules
(   ), 11th, Per pale or and vert a lion rampant gules (Bigod), 12th
Or six lions rampant, two, two, and two sable (Ferrers), 13th, Vairy or
and gules (Ferrers of Chartley), 14th, Azure three garbs or (Chester),
15th, Gules seven mascles conjoined or (Quincy), 16th, Gules a cinquefoil pierced ermine (Beaumont), impaling, Qly, 1st and 4th, Per pale or
and gules three lions passant guardant in pale within a bordure, all
counterchanged (Withypole), 2nd, Qly ermine and gules (Stanhope),
3rd, Azure on a bend wavy or three birds sable beaked gules within a
bordure engrailed argent charged with roundels sable and gules (Rede)
Viscount's coronet   Motto: Basis constantia virtutis
Supporters: Dexter, A talbot argent eared and ducally gorged gules
Sinister, A reindeer proper armed and ducally gorged or
Winged skull below
For Leicester Devereux, 6th Viscount Hereford, who m. 1st, 1642,
Elizabeth, dau. and heir of Sir William Withypole of Ipswich, and d.
Dec. 1676, buried at Sudbourne, 2 Jan. 1677.   (B.P. 1891 ed.;
Corder's 'Christchurch', 32; E.A. Misc. 1911, 62-7; Moore Smith's
'Withypoll'; Mills MS., 90-2)

2. **Dexter background black**
Qly of twenty, 1st, Devereux, 2nd, Gules a lion rampant holding in the
dexter paw a rose, all or (Price of Rhiwlas), 3rd, Bourchier, the cross
sable, 4th, Thomas of Woodstock, 5th, Bohun, 6th, Azure on a bend or
three fleurs-de-lys azure, on a chief or two eagles displayed azure
(Martin), 7th, Withypole, 8th, Stanhope, 9th, Fitzwalter, 10th, Per pale
sable and or an escarbuncle sable (Mandeville), 11th, Gules a fess argent
between six billets or (Lovaine), 12th, Argent a fess and a canton gules
(Widville), 13th, Crophull, 14th, Or a fret gules (   ), 15th, Bigod,
16th, Indecipherable (? Ferrers), 17th, Chester, 18th, Quincy, 19th,
Rede, 20th, Beaumont
Viscount's coronet   Crest: Out of a ducal coronet or a talbot's head
argent eared gules   Mantling: Gules and argent
Motto: Basis virtutis constantia   Supporters: As 1.
For Price Devereux, 10th Viscount Hereford, who m. 1st, 1721, his
cousin Elizabeth, dau. and heir of Leicester Martin, and 2nd, Eleanora,
dau. of Roger Price of Rhiwlas, and d. 27 July 1748.   (Sources, as 1.)

3. **Sinister background black**
Martin, impaling, Devereux   Devereux also in pretence, but on
sinister coat
Crest: A tower chequy or and azure   Mantling: Gules and argent
Motto: Basis virtutis constantia (Devereux)
For Anne, posthumous dau. of Leicester, 6th Viscount Hereford, who
m. 1700, her cousin, Leicester Martin, and d.   (Sources, as 1.)

4. All black background
Martin   In pretence: Devereux
Crest, mantling and motto: As 3.
For Leicester Martin, who m. 1700, Anne, posthumous dau. of
Leicester, 6th Viscount Hereford, and d. 1732.   (Sources, as 1.)

5. Dexter background black
Two roundels   Dexter, within the Garter, Qly, 1st and 4th, Sable on
a bend cotised argent a rose gules between two annulets sable
(Conway), 2nd, qly, i. and iv. Or on a pile gules between six fleurs-de-
lys azure three lions passant guardant or (Seymour augmentation),
ii. and iii. Gules two wings conjoined in lure or (Seymour), 3rd, Ermine
on a fess gules three escallops or, a canton gules (Ingram)   Sinister,
within a garter, but with sprays instead of Garter motto, as dexter with,
in pretence, Qly, 1st (obscured), 2nd, Azure a chevron between three
lions passant or (   ), 3rd (partly obscured) Sable . . . within a
bordure argent (   ), 4th Ingram without canton
Marquess's coronet   Crest: The bust of a Moor in profile, couped at
the shoulders proper, wreathed at the temples argent and sable
Motto: Fide et amore   Supporters: Two Blackamoors, wreathed
about the temples argent and sable habited in golden Roman breast-
plates and buskins, adorned about their waists with green and red
feathers, each holding in the exterior hand a shield azure garnished or,
the dexter charged with a sun in spendour or, the sinister with a crescent or
All on a mantle gules and ermine
For Francis, 2nd Marquess of Hertford, K.G., who m. 2nd, 1776,
Isabella, eldest dau. and co-heir of Charles Ingram, 9th Viscount Irvine,
and d. 28 June 1822.   (B.P. 1949 ed.)
(There is another hatchment for the 2nd Marquess in the parish church
of Arrow, Warwickshire)

6. Dexter background black
Two shields   Dexter, within the Garter, Qly, 1st and 4th, Conway,
and 3rd, qly, i. and iv. Seymour Augmentation, ii. and iii. Seymour
Sinister, within an ornamental wreath, as dexter, impaling, Argent a
double-headed eagle displayed sable (? Fagniani)
Marquess' coronet   Crests: 1. The bust of a Moor in profile, couped
at the shoulders proper, wreathed at the temples argent and azure
2. From a ducal coronet or a phoenix in flames proper   Motto:
Fide et amore
Supporters: As 5.   All on a mantle gules and ermine
For Francis Charles, 3rd Marquess of Hertford, K.G., who m. 1798,
Maria Fagniani, and d. 1 Mar. 1842.   (B.P. 1953 ed.; Copinger, V,
119-20)
(There is another hatchment for the 3rd Marquess in the parish church
at Arrow, Warwickshire)

TANNINGTON

1. Sinister background black
Barry of ten or and sable a bend gules (Barker), impaling, Argent on a
bend between two lions rampant gules three molets or (Ray)
Morto: Spes mea in deo   Cherub's head above shield
For Jane, dau. of Samuel Ray, of Tannington, who m. the Rev. Samuel
Barker, and d. 19 Aug. 1820, aged 27.   (M.I. in church; Palmer's
'Perlustrations of Yarmouth', 401; Farrer MS.)

THEBERTON

1. Sinister background black
Argent two bars between two molets in pale sable (Doughty), impaling,
Barry of ten argent and azure on a canton or a chough proper (Hotham)
Mantle: Gules and ermine   Motto: Palma non sine pulvere
For Frederica, dau. of the Hon. and Rev. Frederick Hotham, Rector of
Donnington, who m. 1840, the Rev. Charles Montagu Doughty of
Theberton Hall, and d. 1843.   (B.L.G. 1900 ed.; Doughty's
'Theberton', 233)
(This hatchment was in fairly good condition in 1955, but has since
been destroyed)

THORINGTON

1. All black background
Argent on a cross between four frets gules a tower argent (Bence)
Crest: A tower argent   Mantling: Gules and argent
Motto: Mors janua vitae
For Alexander Bence, only son of Alexander Bence of Thorington
Hall.   He d. unm., buried at Thorington, 7 June 1742, aged 31.
(Hill's 'Registers of Thorington')

2. Sinister background black
Gules a chevron or between three bezants (Golding)   In pretence:
Argent on a cross gules a tower argent between four frets gules (Bence)
Motto: In coelo quies   Two cherubs' heads above and skull in base
For Anne, dau. and afterwards heir of Alexander Bence of Thorington
Hall, who m. 1762, George Golding of Poslingford and (jure uxoris)
Thorington Hall, and was buried at Thorington, 3 Oct. 1794, aged 80.
(Source, as 1.)

3. All black background
Golding   In pretence: Bence
Crest: A dragon's head erased sable gutty, collared and ringed or
Motto: In coelo quies

For George Golding of Poslingford and Thorington Hall, who m. 1762,
Ann, dau. and heir of Alexander Bence of Thorington Hall, and d.s.p.,
buried at Thorington, 29 Dec. 1803, aged 79.   (Source, as 1.)

THORNHAM MAGNA

1. All black background
On a lozenge   Qly, 1st and 4th, Argent on a cross sable a leopard's
face or (Brydges), 2nd and 3rd, Or a pile gules (Chandos)   In
pretence: Azure three columns of the Corinthian order with balls on
the tops or (Major)
Duchess's coronet   Mantle: Gules and ermine
Supporters: Two otters argent
For Elizabeth, dau. and co-heir of Sir John Major, Bt. of Worlingworth
Hall, who m. 1767, as his 3rd wife, Henry Brydges, 2nd Duke of
Chandos, and d. post 1803.   (B.P. 1868 ed.: Betham's 'Baronetage',
III, 318)
(Husband's hatchment is at Whitchurch, Middlesex)

2. Sinister background black
Major, in centre chief the Badge of Ulster, impaling, Azure on a chevron
or between three hawks rising argent seven roundels gules (Dale)
Motto: Deus major columna   Two cherubs' heads at top corners of
shield and winged skull in base
For Elizabeth, only dau. of Daniel Dale, of Bridlington, Yorks, who m.
1723/4, John Major, later 1st Bt., of Worlingworth and Thornham
Halls, and d. 4 Sept. 1780, aged 76.   (B.P. 1939 ed.; Betham, III,
318; Top. and Gen., II, 246)

3. All black background
Major, with Badge of Ulster in centre chief, impaling Dale
Crest: A dexter arm embowed vested azure cuffed argent holding a
baton or the elbow charged with a roundel argent   Mantle: Gules
and argent
Motto: In coelo quies   Two cherubs' heads at sides and winged skull
below
For Sir John Major, 1st Bt., who m. 1723/4, Elizabeth, only dau. of
Daniel Dale, and d. 16 Feb. 1781, aged 82.   (Sources, as 2)

4. Sinister background black
Qly, 1st and 4th, Major, 2nd and 3rd, qly i. and iv. Or on a chevron
gules between two crescents in chief and an escallop in base azure
three estoiles argent (Henniker), ii. and iii. Major, in centre chief the
Badge of Ulster, impaling, Qly, 1st, Sable a fess or between two swords

palewise proper the first with the point in chief the other with point in
base (Gwynne), 2nd, Or three eagles displayed sable (   ), 3rd, Gules
a lion rampant reguardant or (Gwynne of Garth), 4th, Argent three
boars' heads couped close sable (Glodrydd)
Baroness's coronet   Mantle: Gules and ermine   Supporters:
Dexter, A stag argent attired or gorged with a wreath of oak leaves
fructed proper, pendant therefrom an escutcheon gules charged with
an escallop or   Sinister, An otter argent ducally gorged or, pendent
therefrom an escutcheon with the arms of Major   Cherub's head
above coronet
For Emily, dau. of Robert Jones, of Duffryn, co. Glam., who m. John,
2nd Baron Henniker, and d. 19 Dec. 1819, aged 64.   (B.P. 1891 ed.;
Farrer MS.)

5. All black background
Arms: As 4.
Baron's coronet   Crests: Dexter, An escallop or charged with an
estoile gules   Sinister, Major, as 3.   Mantle: Gules and ermine
Motto: Deus columna major   Supporters: As 4.
For John, 2nd Baron Henniker, who d.s.p. 5 Dec. 1821, aged 68.
(Sources, as 4.)

6. Dexter background black
Qly, 1st and 4th, Major, 2nd and 3rd, Henniker, in fess point the Badge
of Ulster, impaling, Per pale gules and azure a griffin segreant argent, on
a chief engrailed ermine three lozenges azure (Chafy)
Baron's coronet   Crest, mantle, motto and supporters: As 5.
For John Minet Henniker, 3rd, Baron Henniker, who m. 1799, Mary,
eldest dau. of the Rev. William Chafy, Canon of Canterbury, and d.
22 July 1832.   (B.P. 1891 ed.)

7. All black background
On a lozenge   Arms: As 6.
Baroness's coronet   Mantle: Gules and ermine   Supporters:
As 6.
For Mary, widow of John Minet Henniker, 3rd Baron Henniker.   She
d. 10 Jan. 1837.   (B.P. 1891 ed.)

THORPE MORIEUX

1. All black background
Qly, 1st and 4th, Azure two bars ermine between six estoiles, three,
two, one or (Harrison), 2nd and 3rd, Argent three crescents paly of
eight azure and gules (Haynes)   In pretence: Qly, 1st, Chequy argent
and gules on a pale sable three molets or (Fiske), 2nd, Per pale

embattled or and azure (Gosnold), 3rd, Azure a lion rampant guardant
argent (Thomas), 4th, Argent a chevron gules within a bordure engrailed
sable (   )
Crest: A stork wings expanded argent beaked and legged or
Mantling: Gules and argent   Motto: Ferendo et feriendo
For John Haynes Harrison, of Copford Hall, Essex, who m. 1783,
Sarah Thomas, only child of the Rev. John Fiske, Rector of Thorpe
Morieux, and d. 2 Dec. 1839, aged 83.   (Ffiske's 'Fiske Family
Papers', 206 ped., 214)

2. All black background
Per bend argent and gules two bendlets between six roses barbed and
seeded proper all counterchanged, in dexter chief the Badge of Ulster
(Warner), impaling, Qly, 1st and 4th, Azure a lion rampant argent armed
and langued gules (Maude), 2nd and 3rd, Argent three bars gemel sable
over all a lion rampant gules charged with a cross crosslet fitchy or
(De Montalt)
Crest: A Saracen's head affronté couped at the breast, bearded grey,
vested gules, on the head a conical cap chequy argent and gules, on the
breast three roses fesswise argent   Mantling: Gules and argent
Motto: Spero
Pendent from the shield the badge of the Order of the Bath, civil division
For Sir Thomas Courtenay Theydon Warner, 1st Bt. of Brettenham Park,
who m. 1883, Lady Leucha Diana Maude, 6th dau. of the 1st Earl de
Montalt, and d. 15 Dec. 1934.   (B.P. 1953 ed.; gravestone in churchyard)

THRANDESTON

1. All black background
Qly, 1st and 4th, Argent a lion rampant gules semy of trefoils slipped
or, a bordure dovetailed gules (Blakeley), 2nd and 3rd, Azure a fess
between in chief two unicorns' heads erased and in base a cross formy
all or (Rix), impaling, Paly of six or and azure on a chief gules three
martlets or (Martyn)
Crest: A unicorn passant azure gutty or ducally gorged argent, resting
the dexter leg on an inescutcheon or charged with a pale vair
Mantling: Gules and argent   Motto: Allons dieu ayde
Inscribed on frame: John Rix Blakeley—Died June 1810.
Elizabeth Blakeley—died April 1822
For John Rix Blakeley, of Goswold Hall, who m. Elizabeth Martyn,
and d. 9 June 1810, aged 47.   Also for his widow, d. 4 Apr. 1822,
aged 55.   (Partridge's 'Suff. Churchyard Inscriptions', 96)

2. All black background
Identical to No. 1, except for a molet argent in fess point of shield for
difference, and change of motto to 'Resurgam'

Probably for William Rix Blakeley, third son of above, who d. 2 Nov. 1842, aged 49.   (Source, as l.)
(These two hatchments were obviously painted at the same time, being identical in treatment)

LITTLE THURLOW

1. Dexter background black
Gules a chevron between three mallets or, on the chevron a crescent sable for difference (Soame), impaling, Argent three cinquefoils sable a chief azure (Stone)
Crest: On a lure argent and gules a falcon or
Mantling: Gules and argent   Motto: Resurgemus
Inscribed on frame: Sir Stephen Soame, Knt. Died 23rd May 1619
For Sir Stephen Soame, of Little Thurlow, Lord Mayor of London, 1598, who m. Anne, dau. of William Stone, of Segenhoe, Beds, and d. 23 May 1619, aged 75.   (Copinger, V; E.A. N. and Q. (N.S.), III, 247; Misc. Gen. et Her. 5th Ser. VIII, 343, 345)
(This hatchment is not contemporary; perhaps a later copy)

2. All black background
On a lozenge   Arms: As 1.
Inscribed on frame: Dame Anne Soame, Daughter of Wm Stone, Esq., Widow of Sir Steph. Soame, Knt. Died 1622
For Anne, widow of Sir Stephen Soame.   She d. 20 Aug. 1622, aged 67.   (Sources, as 1., but Copinger, I)
(This hatchment is not contemporary; perhaps a later copy)

3. All black background
Soame (no crescent), impaling, Argent two bars and in chief two pallets azure (Churchman)
Crest and mantling: As 1.   Motto: Mors janua vitae
Inscribed on frame: John Soame, Esqr. Died 1709
For John Soame, grandson of 1., who m. Margaret, dau. of Ozias Churchman, of London, and d. 1709.   (B.E.B.; Misc. Gen. et Her. 5th Ser. VIII, 345)

4. All black background
On a lozenge   Soame, as 3. impaling, Azure ten estoiles, four, three, two, one or (Alston)
Motto: In coelo quies   Cherub's head above, skull below
Frame inscribed: Anne Soame, Daughter of Josh. Alston, Esqr. Widow of Stepn. Soame, Esqr. Died 1781

For Anne, 2nd dau. of Joseph Alston, of Edwardstone, who m Stephen
Soame, and d. Jan 1781.   He d. at Reading, 1764, aged 56.
(Misc. Gen. et Her.)

5. **Sinister background black**
Qly, 1st and 4th, Or a pale between two lions rampant sable (Naylor),
2nd and 3rd, Gules two bars and a chief indented or (Hare), impaling,
Alston
Motto: In coelo quies   Cherub's head above, skull below
For Margaret, dau. of Joseph Alston, of Edwardstone, who m. the Rt.
Rev. Dr. Hare, Bishop of Chichester, and d.   (B.E.B.)

TRIMLEY ST. MARTIN

1. **Dexter background black**
Per fess nebuly vert and sable three martlets or a canton ermine, in fess
point the Badge of Ulster (Barker), impaling, Sable three horses' heads
erased argent (Lloyd)
Crest: A bear sejant or collared sable   Mantling: Gules and argent
Motto: In coelo quies   Skull below
For Sir John Fytch Barker, 7th Bt., of Grimston Hall, who m. Lucy,
dau. of Sir Richard Lloyd of Hintlesham, and d.s.p. 3 Jan. 1766, aged
24.
(B.E.B.; Copinger, III, 99-100; E.A. N. and Q. (N.S.), III, 340 and XI,
254, note; Aldred's 'Suff. Records', 83)

2. **All black background**
Qly, 1st, Azure billetty a lion rampant or (Nassau), 2nd, Or a lion
rampant guardant gules ducally crowned azure (Dietz), 3rd, Gules a
fess argent* (Vianden), 4th, Gules two lions passant guardant in pale or
(Catznellogen), on an inescutcheon, Gules three millrinds and in chief a
label of three points argent* (Zuleistein)
Crest: A stag's attire gules issuing from a ducal coronet or
Mantling: Azure and argent*   Motto: Spes durat avorum
*Now sable
For George Richard Savage Nassau, 2nd son of Hon. Richard Savage
Nassau and his wife, Elizabeth Spencer.   He d. unm. 18 Aug. 1823,
aged 67.
(Copinger, III, 100; Aldred's 'Suff. Records', 83-4: Gents. Magazine,
1823, pt. II, 178)
(This hatchment consists of a silken ? banner sewn on to a canvas
backing and then put into a very wide frame. Silver paint tarnished to
black)

UFFORD

1. Sinister background black
Gules on a chevron argent a lion rampant sable crowned or (Brooke)
In pretence: Sable a lion passant guardant or between three saltires
argent (Thompson)
Crest: On a chapeau gules and ermine a wing gules charged with a
chevron argent thereon a lion rampant sable crowned or   Motto: In
ardua virtus
For Anne, dau. and heiress of Samuel Thompson, of Ufford Place, who
m. as his 1st wife, Francis Brooke, of Woodbridge, and d. 20 June,
1772, aged 34.   (Mills MS.; Gage's 'Thingoe Hundred', 391-4; Mon.
in church)

2. Dexter background black
Brooke, impaling to dexter, Thompson, and to sinister, Or three roses
purpure and a chief gules (Sparrow)
Crest: As 1.   Mantling: Gules and argent
Motto: In God my trust   Cherubs' heads at top corners of shield
For Francis Brooke, of Woodbridge, who m. 1st, Anne, dau. and heiress
of Samuel Thompson, of Ufford Place, and 2nd, Mary, dau. of the Rev.
John Sparrow, Rector of Kettleburgh, and d. 3 July 1799, aged 61.
(Sources, as 1.)

3. Sinister background black
Per chevron argent and gules a crescent counterchanged, in centre chief
the Badge of Ulster (Chapman), impaling, Argent a fess dancetty gules
between three eagles displayed sable (Newman)
Crest, mantling and motto, now indistinguishable, owing to bad
condition
For Mary Newman, of Ham Abbey, Essex, who m. 1759, as his 1st
wife, Sir William Chapman, 3rd Bt., and was buried at Ufford, 19 Oct.
1760.   (Sources, as 1.)

4. Dexter background black
Qly, 1st and 4th, Or a chevron sable between three towers gules
(Oneby), 2nd and 3rd, Gules a fess or ermined sable between three
owls or (Webb), impaling, Vairy argent and sable a fess gules (Brace-
bridge)
Crest: A bear's head couped per pale argent and gules
Mantling and motto: now indistinguishable, owing to bad condition
For Robert Oneby, of Loudham Park, who m. 1743, Mary, dau. of
Samuel Bracebridge, and d. 18 June 1753, aged 43.   (Sources, as 1.)

5. All black background
On a lozenge   Arms: As 4.
For Mary, widow of Robert Oneby.   She d.
(All the Ufford hatchments were in bad condition when recorded in
1955. Since then they have deteriorated, and in 1969 No. 5 was in rags
and indecipherable)

WETHERDEN

1. **Sinister background black**
Per fess indented azure and argent (Crawford), impaling, Argent a lion
rampant within a bordure engrailed sable semy of molets argent (Cowley)
Mantling: Gules and argent   Motto: Conquiesco   Cherub's
head above
For Elizabeth Dorothie Cowley, who. m. William Crawford, of
Haughley Park (his hatchment, *see* Haughley 4), and d. 13 Aug. 1828,
aged 69.   (Copinger, VI, 205)

2. **All black background**
On a lozenge   Sable three roses argent (Smythe)   In pretence:
Argent a chevron gules between three pheons points upwards sable
(Sulyard)   Cherub's head above
For Lucy, dau. of Edward Sulyard, who m. Hugh Philip Smythe, and
d. 1830, at Bury.   (E.A. Misc. [1931], 25, and [1932], 86)

3. **Dexter background black**
Sulyard   In pretence: Argent a chevron between three ravens'
heads erased sable (Ravenscroft); and impaling, Azure crusilly and a
lion rampant argent (Dalton)
Crest: A stag's head couped proper attired or   Mantling: Gules and
argent
Winged skull in base
For Edward Sulyard, of Haughley Park, who m. 1st, Susanna, dau. and
co-heiress of George Ravenscroft, of Spalding, Lincs, and 2nd, Dorothy,
dau. of John Dalton, of Thurnham Hall, Lancs, and was buried at
Wetherden, 1 Nov. 1799, aged 55.   (E.A. Misc. [1931], 5, and
[1932], 85-6)

4. **All black background**
On a lozenge   Qly of eight, 1st, Sulyard, 2nd, Barry wavy of eight
or and sable (Fairford), 3rd, Gules on a chief argent two molets pierced
sable (Bacon), 4th, Gules a chevron or between three lions rampant
argent (Good), 5th, Argent on a bend cotised sable three molets argent
(Andrews), 6th, Ermine on a cross gules five escallops or (Weyland),
7th, Gules a rose or (Burnavill), 8th, Argent on a cross sable five
bezants (Stratton)   In pretence (on a lozenge): Ravenscroft   Also
impaling, Dalton, but crusilly and lion rampant or
Mantling: Gules and argent   Skull above
For Dorothy, widow of Edward Sulyard.   She d. 28 May 1830,
aged 82.   (E.A. Misc. [1932], 86)

WILBY

1. Dexter background black

Per pale azure and gules a chevron between three stags trippant or (Green), impaling, Sable a chevron argent between three Moors' heads couped below the shoulder proper, each charged about the neck with a longbow proper   (Hartcup)

Crest: A stag's head erased proper   Mantling: Gules and argent

Motto: Virides fecere merendo   Unframed

For Thomas Green, barrister-at-law, of Wilby, who m. 1795, Catherine, dau. of Lt.-Col. Thomas Hartcup, R.E., and. d. 6 Jan. 1825, aged 55.

(Farrer MS.: Page's 'Suffolk', 433; B.L.G., 1952 ed.)

WISSINGTON

1. Sinister background black

Gules a lion rampant or debruised by a bend argent charged with three crosses formy fitchy azure (Gibbons), impaling, Ermine on a bend cotised sable three boars' heads erased or (Burman)

Mantling: Gules and argent   Motto: In coelo quies

Cherub's head above shield

For Elizabeth, dau. of Thomas Burman, of Smallbridge, who m. as her 2nd husband, Thomas Gibbons, M.D., and d. 20 Feb. 1798.

(Partridge's 'Suffolk Churchyard Inscriptions', 20)

2. Dexter background black

Vert fretty or (Whitmore), impaling, Azure on a fess argent between three pelicans in their piety or three roundels sable (? Pierse or Pearce)

Crest: A falcon sejant on the stump of a tree with a branch springing from the dexter side proper   Mantling: Gules and argent   Motto: Resurgam

Unidentified

Several of the Whitmore family are buried in the churchyard

WITHERSFIELD

1. All black background

Argent on a fess sable between six acorns or three oakleaves vert (Oakes), impaling, Argent a chevron gules between three tigers' heads erased proper (Jacob)

Crest: A stag's head proper   Mantling: Gules and argent

Motto: Robur et vir tute

For the Rev. Abraham Oakes, Rector of Withersfield, who m.
Catherine, dau. of Sir John Jacob, 3rd Bt. of West Wratting, and d.
22 June 1756.
(B.P. 1891 ed.; M.I. in church)
(This is a very small hatchment [c. 2ft. x 2ft.] and it has been very
badly and incorrectly restored)

WOODBRIDGE

1. All black background
Argent three bends gules on a canton azure a spur or (Knight)
Mantling: Azure and or   Motto: Mors janua vitae
Skull and crossbones above shield surmounted by winged hour-glass
Perhaps for Robert or Thomas Knights, surviving sons of Thomas
Knights (who d. 30 Jan. 1707, aged 63) and Mary Goodwin.   (Mills
MS.; mon. slab in church)

2. All red background
On a lozenge surmounted by a skull and crossbones
Knight, impaling, Or a fess between six lions' heads erased gules
(Goodwin)
Mantling: Azure and or   Motto: Mors janua vitae
For Mary, dau. and co-heir of Robert Goodwin of Charsfield, who m.
Thomas Knights, and d.   (Sources, as 1.)

3. Sinister background black
Or a chevron sable between three murrs proper (Carthew), impaling,
Argent a fleur-de-lys gules (Morden)
Mantling: Azure and or   Motto: Mors Janua vitae
Cherub's head above shield
For Elizabeth, dau. and heir of the Rev. Thomas Morden, Rector of
Weston, who m. as the 1st of his four wives, the Rev. Thomas Carthew,
of Woodbridge Abbey, Rector of Woodbridge, and d. 13 Dec. 1768.
(B.L.G. 1853 ed.)

4. Sinister background black
Carthew, impaling, Gules a chevron ermine between three eagles dis-
played argent, on a chief embattled or three roundels sable (Wall)
Crest: A murr proper ducally gorged or   Mantling: Gules and argent
Motto: Per crucem ad stellas   Skull below
For Mary, dau. of Thomas Wall, of Aldeburgh, who m. 1770, as his 2nd
wife, the Rev. Thomas Carthew, of Woodbridge Abbey, and d. June
1771.   (B.L.G. 1953 ed.)

5. **Sinister background black**

Carthew, impaling, Argent a chevron sable between three molets gules (Denny)

Motto: Pono ut resumam   Two cherubs' heads above shield within a sunburst

Winged skull below

For Ann, dau. and co-heiress of Robert Denny, of Eye, who m. 1774, as his 3rd wife, the Rev. Thomas Carthew, and d. 1785.   (B.L.G. 1853 ed.; Topog. and Geneal. II, 504)

6. **Dexter background black**

Qly, 1st and 4th, qly i. and iv. Carthew, ii. and iii. Azure a chevron between three escallops within a bordure engrailed or (Colby), 2nd and 3rd, Argent a fleur-de-lys gules (Morden)   In pretence: Argent on the sea proper an ancient ship at anchor with three masts, sails furled sable, colours flying azure and gules, with the Augmentation of a canton gules charged with a baton or and a sword proper pommel and hilt or encircled by a mural crown argent (Myers)

Crest: A murr proper ducally gorged or   Motto: In Christo fides

For William Carthew, Rear-Admiral, R.N., who m. Pleasance, dau. and co-heir of Graham Thomas Myers, of Dublin, and d. 31 July 1827, aged 70.   (Sources, as 5.)

WORTHAM

1. **All black background**

Azure three quatrefoils argent (Vincent), impaling, Azure a chevron between three escallops or (Colby)

Crest: Out of a ducal coronet or a bear's head argent

Mantling: Gules and argent

Probably used for both Philip Vincent of Marlingford and his 2nd wife, Elizabeth Colby.   He d. 13 Jan. 1724, aged 80; she d. 9 Feb. 1728, aged 72.   (Doughty's 'Betts of Wortham', 169; E.A. Peds. [Harl. Soc.], 227; Farrer's Church Heraldry of Norfolk, I, 275)

2. **All black background**

Sable a bend argent three cinquefoils gules within a bordure engrailed argent (Betts)   In pretence: Betts, with a crescent argent in sinister chief for difference

Crest: From a ducal coronet or a buck's head gules attired or

Mantling: Gules and argent   Motto: Resurgam   Skull and cross-bones in base

For the Rev. George Betts, Rector of Overstrand, Norfolk, who m. 1775, his cousin, Mary, dau. of Edmund Betts, of Oakley, and d. 11 Apr. 1822, aged 71.   (B.L.G. 2nd ed.; Doughty's 'Betts of Wortham')

WRENTHAM

1. Dexter background black
Sable a chevron ermine between three estoiles argent (Brewster), impaling, Chequy or and gules (Malden)
Crest: A bear's head erased azure   Mantling: Gules and argent
Motto: Verite soyet ma garde
For Humphrey Brewster, of Wrentham Hall, who m. Elizabeth Malden, of Fressingfield, and d. 5 Sept. 1735, aged 53.   (B.L.G. 2nd ed.; Rix MS., 'Wrentham History', Brewster ped.; Mills MS.)

2. Dexter background black
Qly, 1st and 4th, Brewster, 2nd and 3rd, Malden, but chequy argent and gules   In pretence: Qly, 1st and 4th, Gules a fess wavy between three lions rampant or (Crompton), 2nd and 3rd, Argent two bars gules on a canton gules a trefoil slipped or (Vincent)
Crest and mantling: As 1.   Motto: In coelo quies
For Philip Brewster, of Wrentham Hall, who m. Isabella Crompton, of Doncaster, and d. 21 Dec. 1765, aged 53.   (B.L.G. 1853, ed.; Sources, as 1.)

YAXLEY

1. All black background
Argent on a saltire engrailed sable nine annulets or (Leeke)
Crest: A peacock's tail displayed proper between two eagles or
Mantling: Gules and argent   Motto: Gloria deo in excelsis
Skull below
Inscribed on Frame: Revd Seymour Leeke, Yaxley Hall, died March 2nd 1786, aged 43 years
For the Rev. Seymour Leeke, of Yaxley Hall, who m. 1772, Mary, dau. of Humphrey Rant, of Dickleburgh, Norfolk, and d. 2 Mar. 1786.
(Proc. S.I.A., XVI, 150-5; Anon. 'Pedigrees of Rant and Freston')

2. All black background
Arms, crest, mantling and motto: As 1.
For Francis Gilbert Yaxley Leeke, illegitimate half-brother of 1. and his heir.   He m. 1818, Ann Osborne, dau. of Charles Clubbe, of Hoxne, and d. 1836.   (Proc. S.I.A., XVI, 147-65)

YOXFORD

1. All black background
Azure on a fess embattled counter-embattled between three goats trippant argent armed or three roundels sable (Mann), impaling, Azure

ten estoiles four, three, two, one or (Alston)
Crest: A demi-dragon gules gutty or   Mantling: Gules and argent
A small hatchment c. 2ft. x 2ft.
For Thomas Mann, of the Inner Temple, and Yoxford, who m.
Elizabeth, dau. of William Alston, of Marlesford, Suffolk, and d. 1669.
She d. and was buried at Yoxford, 17 Feb. 1690/1.   (B.E.B.;
Muskett's 'Suff. Manorial Families', III, 80D)
(Hatchment may have been also used for widow)

2. **Dexter background black**
Sable on a bend argent three cinquefoils gules within a bordure
engrailed or (Betts), impaling, Argent a cross patonce between four
martlets gules, a canton azure (Byrd)
Crest: From a ducal coronet or a stag's head gules attired or collared
argent, the collar charged with three cinquefoils gules
Mantling: Gules and argent   Motto: Ideo invigi lavi
For Thomas Betts, of Yoxford, who m. Avice Byrd, of Royden, and d.
1739.   (Church guidebook; Doughty's 'Betts of Wortham', 177-8;
Mills MS.)

3. **All black background**
Gules a bend vair between two fleurs-de-lys argent, in dexter chief the
Badge of Ulster (Blois)
Crest: A gauntlet proper holding a fleur-de-lys argent
Mantling: Gules and argent   Motto: Resurgam
For Sir Charles Blois, 2nd Bt. of Cockfield Hall, who d. unm. 26 Feb.
1760, aged 29.   (Mills MS.; B.P. 1891 ed.; Top and Gen. I, 491)

4. **Dexter background black**
Blois, with Badge of Ulster in centre chief, impaling, Argent a chevron
sable gutty or between three rabbits' heads couped sable (Rabett)
Crest: A cubit arm in armour proper holding a fleur-de-lys argent
Mantling: Gules and argent   Motto: Je me fie en Dieu
For the Rev. Sir Ralph Blois, 4th Bt., of Cockfield Hall, who m. 1738,
Elizabeth, eldest dau. of Reginald Rabett, of Bramfield, and d. 8 May,
1762, aged 59.   (Mills MS.; B.P. 1781 ed.; Betham's 'Baronetage',
III, 74-5)

5. **Sinister background black**
Argent a chevron between three greyhounds' heads erased gules (Fuller)
In pretence: (on a lozenge) Gules a bend vair, in chief the Badge of
Ulster (Blois), impaling, Argent a chevron sable gutty argent between
three rabbits' heads couped close sable (Rabett)
Mantling: Gules and argent   Motto: In coelo quies
Two cherubs' heads above and winged skull below
For Elizabeth, eldest dau. of Reginald Rabett, of Bramfield, who m. 1st,
1738, the Rev. Sir Ralph Blois, 4th Bt., who d. 1762, and m. 2nd, 1767,
Osborn Fuller, and d. 7 Jan. 1780.   (B.P. 1953 ed.; Mills MS.)

6. Sinister background black
Blois, as 3., with Badge of Ulster in sinister chief, impaling, Argent on a bend azure three garbs or (Ottley)
Mantling: Gules and argent   Motto: Je me fie en Dieu
Two cherubs' heads above
For Lucretia, dau. of Thomas Ottley of St. Kitts, who m. as his 2nd wife, Sir John Blois, 5th Bt., and d. 11 July 1808.   (B.P. 1891 ed.; Mills MS.)

7. All black background
Blois, with Badge of Ulster in centre chief, impaling, Ottley
Crest and motto: As 4.   Mantle: Gules and ermine
Two cherubs' heads at ends of motto scroll and winged skull below
For Sir John Blois, 5th Bt., who d. 17 Jan. 1810.   (B.P. 1891 ed.)

8. Sinister background black
Blois, with Badge of Ulster in centre chief   In pretence: Azure three lions' heads erased within a bordure or charged with eight annulets sable (Price)
Motto: Resurgam   Two cherubs' heads and blue lover's knot above
For Clara, dau. of Jocelyn Price, of Camblesworth Hall, Yorks, who m. 1789, Sir Charles Blois, 6th Bt., and d. 22 Feb. 1847.   (B.P. 1891 ed.)

9. All black background
Blois, with Badge of Ulster in centre chief   In pretence: Price
Crest: As 4.   Mantle: Gules and ermine   Motto: Resurgam
For Sir Charles Blois, 6th Bt., who d. 20 Aug. 1850.   (B.P. 1891 ed.)

10. All black background
Argent a cross engrailed sable between four roundels gules (Clayton), impaling, Argent on a chevron sable three cinquefoils argent (Eyre)
Crest: A unicorn lodged argent, armed and maned or
Mantling: Gules and argent   Motto: Resurgamus
For Elizabeth Eyre, who m. John Clayton of Sibton Park, and d. 16 Mar. 1802, aged 41.   (Tablet in church; 'Yoxford Churchyard Inscriptions', Ips. Ref. Lib.)

SELECT BIBLIOGRAPHY

P. G. Summers, *How to read a Coat of Arms*, (National Council of Social Service, 1967), 17-20.

P. G. Summers, *The Genealogists' Magazine*, vol. 12, No. 13 (1958), 443-446.

T. D. S. Bayley and F. W. Steer, 'Painted Heraldic Panels', in *Antiquaries Journal*, vol. 35 (1955), 68-87.

L. B. Ellis, 'Royal Hatchments in City Churches', in *London and Middlesex Arch. Soc. Transactions* (New Series, vol. 10 1948), 24-40 (contains extracts from a herald-painter's work-book relating to hatchments and eighteenth century funerals).

C. A. Markham, 'Hatchments', in *Northampton & Oakham Architectural Soc. Proceedings*, vol. 20, Pt. 2 (1912), 673-687.

INDEX

Acton, Harriot: 70, 71
Acton, Nathaniel Lee: 126, 127:
Alefounder, Elizabeth: 125
Alexander, John: 91
Alexander, Joseph: 91
Allen, Anne: 51
Almack, Elizabeth: 114
Alston, Anne: 136
Alston, Elizabeth: 143
Alston, Margaret: 136
Amherst, William, 1st Baron: 14
Anderson, Charlotte: 72
Anderson, Henrietta Jane: 81, 82
Arbuthnot, Marcia Emma Georgiana: 26
Arcedeckne, Andrew: 92
Arcedeckne, Catherine: 104
Arkell, Elizabeth: 106
Armine, Anne: 109
Ashburnham, Bertram, 4th Earl of: 72
Assheton, Mary: 19
Astley, Blanche: 40
Astley, Mary: 11
Asty, Honor: 97
Atkyns, Harriet: 29
Atkyns: 30
Atwood, Anne: 75
Aufrere, Anthony: 28
Auriol, Amelia: 93

Bacon, Sir Edmund (4th Bt.): 121
Bacon, Sir Edmund (6th Bt.): 121
Bacon, Elizabeth: 121
Bacon, The Rev. Nicholas: 84
Bacon, Nicholas: 83
Bacon: 84, 124
Baden, Princess Mary of: 89
Bagge, Charles Elsden: 13
Bagge, Jane: 7
Baillie, Katharine Charlotte: 72
Baines, Violet Sophia Mary: 45
Baker, Elizabeth: 128
Baker, Sophia: 34

Ballow, Prisca: 121
Barber, Mary: 115
Barclay, Margaret: 60
Barker, Lt.-Col. John: 83
Barker, Sir John Fytch (7th Bt.): 136
Barker, The Rev. Samuel: 131
Barkham, Alice: 49
Barnardiston, Anne: 128
Barnardiston, Arthur: 79, 80
Barnardiston, Nathaniel: 110
Barnardiston, Sir Robert (4th Bt.): 110
Barnardiston, Samuel: 79
Barnardiston, Sir Samuel (1st Bt.): 79
Barnardiston, Sir Samuel (5th Bt.): 110
Barnardiston, Thomas: 110
Barnardiston, Sir Thomas (1st Bt.): 109
Barnardiston, Sir Thomas (2nd Bt): 109
Barnardiston, Sir Thomas (3rd Bt.): 109
Barne, Lt.-Col. Michael: 125
Barne, Miles: 124, 125
Barnwell, The Rev. Charles: 8
Barrett, Nathaniel: 81
Bayning, Henry, 3rd Baron: 24
Beale, Jane: 119
Beauchamp-Proctor, Sir Thomas (2nd Bt.): 31
Beauchamp-Proctor, Sir William (1st Bt.): 31
Beauchamp-Proctor, Sir William (3rd Bt.): 32
Beauclerk, Henrietta Mary: 99
Beckford, Harriet: 92
Beckford, Susan Euphemia: 88
Bedingfeld, Henriette Elizabeth: 8
Bedingfeld, Sir Richard (5th Bt.): 37
Bedingfield, John James: 74
Beevor, Anna Bettina: 22

Beevor, Charlotte: 55
Beevor, Sir Thomas (1st Bt.): 22
Beevor, Sir Thomas (2nd Bt.): 22
Belasyse, Lady Anne: 127
Belasyse, Lady Elizabeth: 90
Bence, Alexander: 131
Bence, Ann: 131, 132
Bence, Katherine: 110
Bence, Lawrence: 101
Berners, Henry, 10th Baron: 30
Berney, Augustus: 10
Berney, Caroline: 35
Berney, Frances: 16
Berney, John: 9
Berney, Robert: 55
Berney, Thomas: 9
Berney, Thomas Trench: 10
Bertie, Lady Georgiana Charlotte:
25, 26
Betts, The Rev. George: 141
Betts, Mary: 141
Betts, Thomas: 143
Birch, Phoebe Ann: 84
Biscoe, Catherine Frances: 21
Blackborne, Anne: 40
Blackerby, Anne: 79
Bladwell, Maria Barbara: 47
Bladwell: 47
Blagrave, Catherine: 82
Blake, Thomas: 42
Blakeley, John Rix: 134
Blakeley, William Rix: 135
Blakeway, Ann: 45
Blofeld, John: 27
Blofeld, Sarah: 27
Blofeld, Thomas: 27
Blofeld, The Rev. Thomas Cal-
thorpe: 27
Blois, Sir Charles (2nd Bt.): 143
Blois, Sir Charles (6th Bt.): 144
Blois, Sir John (5th Bt.): 144
Blois, Lucy Anne: 104
Blois, Mary: 51
Blois, The Rev. Sir Ralph (4th Bt.):
143
Blosse, Mary: 73
Boileau, John Peter: 47

Boileau, Sir John Peter (1st Bt.):
30
Bolton, Mary Katherine: 69
Bolton: 69
Boucherett, Mary: 125
Bracebridge, Mary: 137
Brand, Jacob: 119
Brand, Thomasine: 79
Brand, William Beale: 119
Brand: 119
Branthwayt, Elizabeth: 22
Brewster, Humphrey: 142
Brewster, Philip: 142
Brickwood, Mary Anne: 106
Bristowe, Elizabeth: 9
Britiffe, Judith: 8, 9
Brograve, Sir Berney (Bt.): 56
Broke-Middleton, Sir George Nath-
aniel (3rd Bt.): 72
Bromley, Nathaniel Warner: 80
Brooke, Francis: 137
Brooksbank, Amelia: 41
Brown, Dr. Thomas: 78
Browne, Anna Maria: 84
Browne, Charlotte: 83
Browne, Mary: 17
Browne, Pleasance: 40
Browne, The Rev. Richard: 16
Browne: 54
Brownrigg, Robert: 73
Brydges, Ann: 51
Brydges, Henry (2nd Duke of
Chandos): 132
Buck, The Rev. John Parmenter:
49
Buckinghamshire, John, 1st Earl of:
8, 9
Buckle, Frances: 12, 13
Bulwer, Henry Lytton Earle (Baron
Dalling and Bulwer): 23
Bulwer, William Earle: 18
Bulwer, William Earle Lytton: 23
Bulwer, William Wiggett: 18
Bunbury, Ann: 104
Bunbury, William: 92
Burkin, Diana: 57
Burman, Elizabeth: 139

Burrell, The Hon. Lindsey Merrik
 Peter: 102
Burroughes, The Rev. Ellis: 32
Burroughes, Jeremiah: 57
Burroughes, Randall: 57
Burroughes, The Rev. Randall: 32
Burroughes, Mary: 47
Burroughes: 57
Burton, Mary Elizabeth: 34
Butler, Hon. Jane: 91
Butt, Arabella: 58
Buxton, John: 48
Byrd, Avice: 143
Byrd, Sarah: 81

Calthorpe, Henry, 1st Baron: 68
Calthorpe, Judith: 23
Campbell, Charlotte: 99
Capper, Mary: 116
Carpenter, Frances: 68
Carter, Harriet: 81
Carthew, The Rev. Thomas: 140,
 141
Carthew, Rear-Adm. William: 141
Caton, Elizabeth: 36
Cecil, Edward (1st Viscount Wim-
 bledon): 108
Chafy, Mary: 133
Chambers: 16
Chandos, Henry, 2nd Duke of:
 132
Chapman, Sir William (3rd Bt.):
 137
Charlton, Elizabeth: 105
Cheeke, Elizabeth: 110
Chevallier, The Rev. Temple: 69
Cholmondeley, George, 2nd Mar-
 quess of: 26
Cholmondeley, George Horatio
 Charles, 5th Marquess of: 27
Cholmondeley, George James, 1st
 Marquess of: 25
Cholmondeley, William Henry
 Hugh, 3rd Marquess of: 26
Churchill, Sophia: 53
Churchman, Margaret: 135
Clark, Elizabeth: 110

Clarke, Judith: 42
Clarke, Mary: 7
Clarke, Rebecca: 112
Clayton, John: 144
Cleveland, William John Frederick,
 3rd Duke of: 123
Clive, Hon. Rebecca: 86
Clubbe, Ann Osborne: 142
Cobb, Elizabeth: 21
Cobbold, Katherine Georgina: 105
Cochrane, Anne: 112
Coke, Thoms William (1st Earl of
 Leicester): 48
Colborne, Nicholas, 1st Baron: 20
Colby, Elizabeth: 141
Coldham, Henry Walter: 6
Coldham, James: 5
Coldham, John: 5
Collett: 52
Colman, 78
Colombine, The Rev. Paul: 38
Colvile, The Rev. Nathaniel: 86
Cony, Edwin: 50
Cony, Robert: 49
Conyers, Caroline: 83
Cooke, Vere: 85
Cooke, Sir William (1st Bt.): 11
Cooper, The Rev. Samuel Lovick:
 58
Cornwallis, James, 5th Earl: 59
Corrance, Elizabeth: 119
Corrance, Mary: 119
Cotton, Dr. Ralph: 86
Cowley, Elizabeth Dorothie: 95,
 138
Cowper, Mary: 89
Crane, Elizabeth: 121
Crane, William: 73
Crawford, William: 95, 138
Cremer, Frances: 7
Cresacre: 117
Cresswell, Bridget: 114
Crisp, Major Raymond John
 Steffe: 30
Crompton, Isabella: 142
Cropley, Anne: 121
Cruttenden, Elizabeth: 85

Cubitt, Edward George: 24
Cubitt, Emma: 24
Cubitt, Thomas: 24
Cunningham, Rear-Adm. Sir
  Charles: 89
Cust, Hon. Anne: 71, 85
Custance, Susanna: 43

Dale, Elizabeth: 132
Dalling, Gen. Sir John (1st Bt.): 15
Dalling, Sir William (2nd Bt.): 15
Dalling and Bulwer, Henry Lytton
  Earle, Baron: 23
Dalton, Dorothy: 138
Daniell, Frances: 102
Darcy, Hon. Elizabeth: 113
Daubuz, Mary Anne: 103
Davis, Mary Ann: 31
Davy, John: 23
Day, Mary: 117
Death, Elizabeth: 101
Denny, Ann: 141
Denton, Anne: 57
Devereux, Hon. Anne: 129
Devereux, Leicester (6th Viscount
  Hereford): 129
Devereux, Price (10th Viscount
  Hereford): 129
de Visme, Elizabeth: 93
D'Eye, Mary: 29
D'Eye, Nathaniel: 89
Dillon, Hon. Frances: 36
Discipline, Thomas: 118
Dolens, Margaret: 9
Doughty, The Rev. Charles Mon-
  tagu: 131
Douglas-Hamilton, Alexander (10th
  Duke of Hamilton): 88
Douglas-Hamilton, James (5th
  Duke of Hamilton): 87
Douglas-Hamilton, William (11th
  Duke of Hamilton): 89
Drummond, Adelaide: 99
Drury, Anne: 5
Durrant, Davy: 43
Durrant, Sir Henry Thomas Es-
  tridge (3rd Bt.): 43

Durrant, Margaret: 43
Durrant, Sir Thomas (1st Bt.): 43
Durrant, Sir Thomas (2nd Bt.): 43
Durrant: 42, 43

Earle, Mary: 18
Edgar, Catherine: 13
Edgar, Mileson: 105, 106
Edgar, The Rev. Mileson Gery: 106
Edgar, Mirabella: 78
Edgar, Robert: 108
Edgar, Susannah: 106
Egerton, Lady Frances: 58
Elliot, Lady Catherine Sarah: 30
Ellis, Elizabeth Maria: 32
Else, Mary: 11
Elwes: 37
Evans, Albinia Maria: 72
Eyre: Elizabeth; 144
Eyton, Sarah: 92

Fagniani, Maria: 130
Fairfax, Hon. Margaret: 92
Farr, Georgiana: 101
Farr, Thomas: 117
Fawkener, Mary: 53
Fellowes, Emma: 24
Felton, Frances: 59
Fergus, Mary: 98
Fielding, Lady Mary: 86
Finch, William Finch: 22
Fisher, Helen Sophia: 77
Fiske, Mary: 69
Fiske, Sarah Thomas: 134
Fitzalan-Howard, Bernard (12th
  Duke of Norfolk): 90
Fitzherbert, Charlotte: 99
Flower, Clarissa: 118
Foley, Hon. Georgiana: 18
Folkes, Dorothy: 21
Fonnereau, Rev. Charles William:
  105
Fonnereau, The Rev. Dr. Claudius:
  104
Fonnereau, The Rev. William: 104
Fonnereau, William Charles: 105
Forrest, Cecilia Frederica: 17

Fountaine, Andrew: 35
Fowle, John: 11
Fowle, Sarah: 28
Fowle: 12
Framlingham, Catherine: 55
Frampton, The Rev. Thomas: 117
Fuller, Mary: 6, 143
Fuller, Osborne: 81

Gage, John: 126
Gage, Sir Thomas (3rd Bt.): 98
Gage, Sir Thomas (6th Bt.): 99
Gage, Sir Thomas Rookwood (5th Bt.): 98
Gage, Sir William (2nd Bt.): 80
Gardner, Hon. Charlotte Susannah: 20
Garrard, Mary: 124
Garrard: 33
Gascoyne, Emily: 23
Gawdy, Sir Charles: 85
Gawdy, Sir Charles (1st Bt.): 86
Geary, Mary: 46
George V, H.M. King: 42
George VI, H.M. King: 42
Gery, Susanna: 108
Gibbes, Matilda Lavinia: 10
Gibbons, Thomas: 139
Gibson, Jane: 113
Gilstrap, Sir William (1st Bt.): 90
Goate, Sarah Dionesse: 78
Golding, George: 131, 132
Gooch, Sir Edward Sherlock (6th Bt.): 75
Gooch, Georgiana; 117
Gooch, Sir Thomas (3rd Bt.): 75
Gooch, Sir Thomas (4th Bt.): 74
Gooch, Sir Thomas Sherlock (5th Bt.): 74
Gooch: 74, 75
Goodwin, Anne: 116
Goodwin, John: 115
Goodwin, Mary: 140
Goodwin, William: 116
Gordon, Charlotte: 55
Gould, Henrietta: 100
Gould, Maria Catherine: 103

Graeme, Anne: 48
Graves, Hon. Anne Elizabeth: 46
Green, Elizabeth: 23
Green, Thomas: 17, 129
Greenwood, Mary: 11
Gregg, Mary: 45, 46
Gregory, Anne: 32
Grose, Mary Caroline: 27
Grubb, Mary: 123
Gunton: 33
Gurney, Daniel: 40
Gurney, Hudson: 60
Gurney, John: 15

Haigh, Elizabeth: 90
Halcott, Jane: 56
Hale, Ann: 108
Hales, Elizabeth: 5
Hales, Robert: 6
Hallett: 41
Halliday, Robert: 90
Hallifax, Thomas: 94
Hamby, Katherine: 111
Hamby, Robert: 107
Hammond, Francis: 97
Hammond: 108
Hamond, Sir Andrew Snape (1st Bt.): 48
Hamond, Anne: 96
Hamond, Philip: 53, 96, 114
Hanford, Dorothy Maria: 126
Harbord, Edward (3rd Baron Suffield): 20
Harbord, Edward Vernon (4th Baron Suffield): 20
Harbord, Harbord: 19
Harbord, Harbord (1st Baron Suffield): 19
Harbord, William Assheton (2nd Baron Suffield): 19
Hare, Anne: 22
Hare, Sir Thomas (1st Bt.): 46
Hare, Sir Thomas (4th Bt.): 46
Hare, The Rt. Rev. Dr. Hare: 136
Harrison, John Haynes: 134
Harrison, Susan: 70
Hartcup, Catherine: 139

Hartwell, Robert: 5
Hase, Edward: 41
Hase, Vertue: 41
Hawker, Jane: 56
Haworth, Margaret: 51
Hay, Lady Harriet Jemima: 40
Hay-Drummond, The Very Rev.
  Edward Auriol: 93
Hayes, Laura: 59
Hayward, Anna Maria: 74
Heigham, The Rev. Henry: 103
Heigham, John Henry: 103
Henley, Catherine: 45
Henniker, John, 2nd Baron: 133
Henniker, John Minet, 3rd Baron:
  133
Henshaw, Louisa: 73
Hereford, Leicester, 6th Viscount:
  129
Hereford, Price, 10th Viscount:
  129
Hertford, Francis, 2nd Marquess of:
  130
Hertford, Francis Charles, 3rd Mar-
  quess of: 130
Hervey, Lady Sophia: 17
Hicks, Sarah: 17
Hicks, The Rev. William: 52
Hoare, Samuel (1st Viscount
  Templewood): 44
Hobart, Lady Caroline: 19
Hobart, Sir John (2nd Bt.): 58
Hobart, John (1st Earl of Bucking-
  hamshire): 8, 9
Hobart: 16
Hodgson, Sarah: 69
Holl: 59
Hollond, The Rev. Edmund: 75
Holt, Sir John: 121
Holt, Rowland: 121, 122
Holt, Thomas: 122
Hooke: 33
Hotham, Frederica: 131
Houghton, Rachel: 5
Howard, Julia Barbara: 36
Howe, Dorothy: 50
Howland, George: 95

Howman: 24
Hunter, R. J.: 45
Huntingfield, Joshua, 1st Baron:
  104
Huntingfield, Joshua, 2nd Baron:
  104
Hussey, Frances: 76

Ibbetson, Harriet: 100
Ingram, Hon. Isabella: 130
Ireland, Thomas James: 117
Ives, Hannah: 14
Ives, Jeremiah: 12, 13

Jackson, Elizabeth: 9
Jacob, Catherine: 140
Jacob, Elizabeth: 48
Jacob, Susan: 87
James, Lucy Caroline: 122
Jennens, Mary: 80
Jenney, Arthur: 78
Jermy, John: 6
Jermyn, Hon. Merelina: 80
Jerningham, Charlotte Georgiana:
  37
Jerningham, Edward: 35
Jermingham, Sir William (6th Bt.):
  36
Jodrell, Richard Paul: 41, 42
Johnson, Christabella: 29
Johnson, Letitia: 31
Johnson, Maria: 16
Jones, Emily: 132

Keble, John: 93
Keene, Elizabeth: 54
Kemp, Letitia: 121
Keppel, Lady Anne Amelia: 48
Kerridge, Samuel: 124
Kerridge, Thomas: 91, 124
Kerrison, Mary: 77, 78
Kerrison, Sir Roger: 31
King, Elizabeth: 109
Knatchbull, Eleanor: 16
Knight, Elizabeth: 54
Knight, Lucy: 98, 126
Knights, Mary: 115

Knights, Robert: 140
Knights, Thomas: 140
Knipe, Edmund: 47

Langford, H. S. E. C.: 33
Langley, Mary: 78
Lawford, Louisa: 15
Leathes, George: 101
Leathes, John: 101
Lee, George: 13
Lee, Henry: 80
Leeke, Francis Gilbert Yaxley: 142
Leeke, The Rev. Seymour: 142
Lee-Warner, Anne: 13
Lee-Warner, Daniel Henry: 51
Lee-Warner, The Rev. Daniel
    Henry: 51
Lee-Warner, Henry: 50, 51
Leicester, Thomas William, 1st Earl
    of: 48
Leigh, The Rev. William: 38
Leman, The Rev. Naunton Thomas:
    81, 82
Le Neve, Francis: 40
Le Neve, Peter: 39
L'Estrange, Armine: 45
Life, Mary: 32
Lloyd, Capt. Heneage: 102
Lloyd, Lucy: 136
Lock, Elizabeth: 94
Logan, R. H.: 113
Lombe, Sir John (1st Bt.): 12
Long, Israel: 119
Longe, The Rev. John: 83
Lowther, Lady Caroline: 123
Lukin, Sarah: 17
Lund, Elizabeth: 77
Lygon, Lady Maud: 44
Lynch, Athaliah; 106
Lynch, Williem: 106
Lyne-Stephens, S.: 34
Lytton, Elizabeth Barbara: 18, 19

Maitland, Mary Anne: 128
Maitland, Mary Fuller: 127
Major, Elizabeth: 132
Major, Sir John (1st Bt.): 132

Malden, Elizabeth: 142
Mann, Thomas: 143
Manners, Thomas, 1st Baron: 91
Marsh, Sarah Nasmyth: 32
Marshall: 117
Martin, The Rev. Charles: 118
Martin, Eleanor: 116
Martin, Elizabeth: 129
Martin, Leicester: 129
Martin, Richard Bartholomew: 98
Martin, Tamworth: 126
Martin, William: 98
Martin: 97
Martyn, Elizabeth: 134
Maude, Lady Leucha Diana: 134
Merry, Anthony: 101
Metcalfe, Emma: 96
Metcalfe, Henry: 97
Metcalfe, Lucy: 96
Middleton, Emily: 35
Middleton, Sir William Fowle (1st
    Bt.): 70
Middleton, Sir William Fowle
    Fowle (2nd Bt.): 71, 84
Miller, Elizabeth: 7
Miller, Susanna: 127
Milles, George John (4th Baron
    Sondes): 16
Milles, Mary: 50
Mills, The Rev. Thomas: 128
Mingay, Anna Eliza: 39
Mingay, Anne: 11
Minshull: 107
Mitford, Susan: 14
Molineux-Montgomerie, Thomas:
    18
Moore, Mary: 101
Morden, Elizabeth: 140
Morrice, Ann: 79, 80
Moseley, Sarah Elizabeth: 90
Mott, Thomas: 7
Musgrave: 52
Myers, Pleasance: 141

Nassau, George Richard Savage:
    136
Nassau, Hon. Henry: 87

Nassau, Hon. Richard Savage: 87
Nassau, William Henry (5th Earl of
  Rochford): 88
Neale, Frances: 52
Neale, Harriette Deborah: 105
Neale, Col. Thomas: 105
Negus, Henry: 28, 29
Negus, Sarah: 27
Neville, Sir Reginald James (1st
  Bt.): 45
Newby, Rosamond: 46
Newman, Mary: 137
Norfolk, Bernard, 12th Duke of: 90
Norris, Anne: 28
Norton, Thomas: 59
Nourse, Elizabeth Johanna: 54

Oakes, Abraham: 140
Ogilvie, Gen. George: 47
Oliver, John: 96, 114
Oneby, Robert: 137
Orford, George, 3rd Earl of: 25
Orford, Horace, 4th Earl of: 25,
  53
Orford, Horatio, 2nd Earl of: 25,
  53
Orford, Horatio, 3rd Earl of: 53
Orford, Robert, 2nd Earl of: 25
Orgill, The Rev. Naunton Thomas:
  81
Ottley, Lucretia: 144

Packe, Anne: 53
Palgrave, Christian: 28
Palmer, Mary: 31, 32
Parker, Adm. Sir George: 58
Parker, Sir Henry (6th Bt.): 114
Parker, Sir Hyde (8th Bt.): 115
Parker, John Oxley: 113
Parker, Sir William (7th Bt.): 114
Parsons, Frances: 122
Paston, Edward: 7
Paston, Margaret Anne: 38
Paston-Bedingfeld, Sir Henry
  Richard (6th Bt.): 38
Peach, Nathaniel William: 29
Pearse, Laura Elizabeth: 15

Peckham: 59
Penrice, Hannah: 35
Penrice, Mary: 10
Penrice, Thomas: 38
Piersy, Sarah: 74
Pitcairn, Dr. David: 114
Plestow, Charles Berners: 52
Plestow: 52
Plume, Edmund: 96
Pocklington, Pleasance: 82
Pocklington, Sir Robert: 82
Pocklington, Robert: 82
Pocklington, Samuel: 82
Poley, George Weller: 76, 77
Poley, The Rev. John Weller: 76
Poley, Robert: 77
Poley, The Rev. William Weller: 76
Pollard, Catherine: 122
Pollen, Henrietta: 47
Porter, Jane: 91, 124
Potter, Mary: 93
Powell, Gwendoline: 123
Powlett, Henry (3rd Baron Bayn-
  ing): 24
Pratt, Edward: 40
Pratt, Edward Roger: 40
Pratt, Maria: 6
Pratt, Mary: 28
Preedy, Emilia: 46
Prescott, Louisa Anna Maria: 75
Preston, The Rev. George: 8
Preston, Sir Thomas Hulton (1st
  Bt.): 7
Price, Clara: 144
Price, Eleanora: 129
Purvis, Charles: 85
Pykarell, Pleasance: 82

Rabett, Elizabeth: 77, 143
Rabett, Reginald: 77, 78
Ramell, Caroline: 55
Randall, Anne: 57
Rant, Humphrey: 32
Rant, Jane: 19
Rant, Mary: 142
Ravenscroft, Susanna: 138
Rawle, Lydia: 41

Rawlinson, Susanna: 95
Ray, Elizabeth: 95
Ray, Jane: 131
Ray, The Rev. Richard: 94
Ray, Richard: 94
Reade, Charles Crofts: 70
Reade, John: 102
Rede, Robert: 72, 73
Rede, Sarah Lemon: 58
Reed, James: 107
Repps, Vertue: 41
Reynardson, Mary: 79
Richardson, Harriet: 96, 114
Richardson, Thomas: 113
Rissowe, Charles Thomas: 116
Robarts, Marianne: 18
Roberts, Elizabeth Mary: 107
Robinson, Isabella Esther: 75
Robinson, John: 125
Robinson, Lt.-Gen. John: 86
Robinson, John Nevill: 86
Robinson, William Henry: 86
Rochford, William Henry Nassau,
    5th Earl of: 88
Rolfe, Edmund: 21
Rolle, Margaret: 25
Rookwood, Elizabeth: 126
Rookwood, Thomas: 126
Rookwood-Gage, Sir Edward (9th
    Bt.): 99
Rookwood-Gage, Sir Thomas (8th
    Bt.): 99
Rothwell, Anne: 109, 110
Rowley, Sarah: 98
Rumsey, Mary: 73
Rushbrooke, Robert: 123
Rycroft, Penelope: 126, 127

Salmon, William Orton: 12
Sampson, Bridget: 111
Sassoon, Sybil Rachel Betty Cecile:
    27
Savage, Thomas, 1st Viscount: 113
Say, William: 14
Sayer, John: 89
Service, Elizabeth: 113
Service, Nancy: 113

Severne, Samuel Amy: 120
Seymour-Conway, Francis (2nd
    Marquess of Hertford): 130
Seymour-Conway, Francis Charles
    (3rd Marquess of Hertford): 130
Sharpe, The Rev. Charles Sharpe:
    116
Sharpe, Charles Thomas: 116
Sharpe, Samuel: 82
Shaw, Col. Geoffrey Reginald
    Devereux: 44
Sheriffe, The Rev. Thomas: 101
Shirley, Emily Harriot: 20
Shuldham, William: 115
Skinner: 89
Skottowe, Katharine: 38
Sleorgin, Thomas: 100
Smith, Henry: 16
Smyth, Anna Mirabella Henrietta:
    119
Smyth, John: 49
Smythe, Hugh Philip: 138
Snell, Mary: 100
Soame, John: 135
Soame, Stephen: 136
Soame, Sir Stephen: 135
Somerset, Lady Susan: 26
Sondes, George, 4th Baron: 16
Sparrow, Catherine: 8
Sparrow, Mary: 137
Spencer, Anne: 87
Spencer, Catharine: 24
Spencer, Mary: 27
Spring, Merelina: 118
Spring, Sir Thomas (3rd Bt.): 80
Spring, Sir William (4th Bt.): 80
Stackhouse, The Rev. John: 37
Stafford, George William, 8th
    Baron: 36
Stafford, Henry Valentine, 9th
    Baron: 36
Starkey, Mary: 6
Starkie, Nicholas: 13
Staunton, Anna Maria: 94
Steele, Charlotte: 20
Steenbergen, Sarah Crooke: 43
Stone, Anne: 135

Stone, Robert: 7
Stracey, Diana Julia: 43
Stuart, Elizabeth Jane: 39
Stuart, Mary: 11
Styleman, The Rev. Armine: 45
Styleman, Henry: 45, 46
Styleman, Nicholas: 21, 45
Styles, Elizabeth Joanna: 110
Suckling, Maurice William: 55
Suckling, William: 73
Suffield, Edward, 3rd Baron: 20
Suffield, Edward Vernon, 4th
   Baron: 20
Suffield, Harbord, 1st Baron: 19
Suffield, William Assheton, 2nd
   Baron: 19
Sulyard, Edward: 138
Sulyard, Lucy: 138
Sulyarde, Frances Henrietta: 36
Surtees, Matilda Louisa: 122
Sutton, Sir Richard (2nd Bt.): 34
Symonds, Elizabeth: 103

Tanner, Thomas: 93
Temple, Dorothy: 83
Templewood, Samuel, 1st Vis-
   count: 44
Thellusson, Anne: 17
Theobald, John Medows: 100
Thomas, George: 111, 112
Thompson, Anne: 137
Thompson, Maria: 104
Thornhill, Mary: 124
Thorrowgood, Mary: 124
Thorrowgood, John: 111
Thorrowgood, Katherine: 111
Thorrowgood, Sir Thomas: 111
Thurlow, Edward, 2nd Baron: 69
Thurlow, Edward, 4th Baron: 69
Thurlow, Edward Thomas, 3rd
   Baron: 69
Tomlinson: 33
Tower, Jane: 31
Townshend, John, 4th Marquess:
   39
Tramell, Grace: 115
Trench, Susan: 9

Trotman, Robert: 107
Trusson, Gabriel: 110
Trusson, Thomas: 111
Tunstall, Catherine: 53
Turner, Sir Charles (1st Bt.): 51
Turner, Elizabeth: 50
Turner, Sir John (2nd Bt.): 51
Turner, Sir John (3rd Bt.): 52
Tyrell, Charles: 95
Tyrell, The Rev. Charles: 128
Tyrell, Edmund: 92
Tyrell, Grace: 89
Tyssen, Samuel: 34
Tyssen, Sarah: 55
Tyssen: 14

Usborne, Henry: 84

Vane, William John Frederick (3rd
   Duke of Cleveland): 123
Vanneck, Sir Gerard (2nd Bt.): 103
Vanneck, Sir Joshua (1st Bt.): 103
Vanneck, Joshua (1st Baron Hun-
   tingfield): 104
Vanneck, Joshua (2nd Baron Hun-
   tingfield): 104
Vere, Harriet: 75
Verner, Juliana: 98
Vernon, Hon. Georgiana: 20
Vernon, Leveson: 68
Vincent, Judith: 119
Vincent, Philip: 141
Vincent: 57

Walklate, Margaret: 94
Wall, Mary: 140
Walpole, Francis: 54
Walpole, George (3rd Earl of
   Orford): 25
Walpole, Horace (4th Earl of
   Orford): 25, 53
Walpole, Horatio (2nd Earl of
   Orford): 53
Walpole, Horatio (3rd Earl of
   Orford): 53
Walpole, Robert (2nd Earl of
   Orford): 25

Ward, Frances: 83
Ward, Richard: 41
Ward, Robert: 41
Wardell, Elizabeth: 107
Warner, Sir Thomas Courtenay
  Theydon (1st Bt.): 134
Washington, Elizabeth: 122
Welby, Elizabeth: 117
Welford, Emma: 128
Wellesley, Hon. Georgiana Char-
  lotte Mary: 23
Weston, Col. Thomas: 120
Weyland, John: 54
Weyland, Richard: 55
Whaley, Jane: 76
Whish, Frances Jane: 97
Whitaker, Charles: 108
White, Hester: 29
White, Snowden: 119
Whitmore: 139
Whittaker, Marianne: 74
Wilkins, The Rev. David: 92
Williams, Anne: 104
Wilson, Adm. George: 122
Wilson, George Holt: 122
Wilson, George Rowland Holt: 123
Wilson, George St. Vincent: 122

Wilson, The Rev. Henry (10th
  Baron Berners): 30
Wilson, Henry: 127
Wilson, Joseph: 128
Wimbledon, Edward Cecil, 1st
  Viscount: 108
Windham, Col. William: 17
Windham, The Rt. Hon. William: 17
Windham, Vice-Adm. William: 17
Windham, William Howe: 17
Wingfield, Sir Richard (2nd Bt.):
  87
Withypole, Elizabeth: 129
Wombwell, Sir George (1st Bt.): 95
Wombwell, Sir George (2nd Bt.):
  127
Wood, Sarah: 82
Wrench, Mary: 6
Wrench: 19
Wright, Elizabeth: 5
Wright, Sarah: 80
Wynne, Catherine: 110

Yelloly, Dr. John: 55
Yelloly, Sarah Boddicott: 120

Zouch, Sophia: 108